# Missing Men

Also by Joyce Johnson

JOYCE JOHNSON

# Missing Men

A MEMOIR

VIKING

VIKING
Published by the Penguin Group
Penguin Group (USA) Inc., 375 Hudson Street,
New York, New York 10014, U.S.A.
Penguin Books Ltd, 80 Strand, London WC2R ORL, England
Penguin Books Australia Ltd, 250 Camberwell Road, Camberwell,
Victoria 3124, Australia
Penguin Books Canada Ltd, 10 Alcorn Avenue,
Toronto, Ontario, Canada M4V 3B2
Penguin Books India (P) Ltd, 11 Community Centre, Panchsheel Park,
New Delhi–110 017, India
Penguin Books (N.Z.) Ltd, Cnr Rosedale and Airborne Roads, Albany,
Auckland, New Zealand
Penguin Books (South Africa) (Pty) Ltd, 24 Sturdee Avenue,
Rosebank, Johannesburg 2196, South Africa

Penguin Books Ltd, Registered Offices: 80 Strand, London WC2R ORL, England

First published in 2004 by Viking Penguin, a member of Penguin Group (USA) Inc.

1   3   5   7   9   10   8   6   4   2

Photographs from the author's collection.

LIBRARY OF CONGRESS CATALOGING IN PUBLICATION DATA
Johnson, Joyce, 1935–
Missing men: a memoir / Joyce Johnson
p.  cm.
ISBN 0-670-03310-3
1. Johnson, Joyce, 1935—Family. 2. Johnson, Joyce, 1935—Marriage.
3. Johnson, Joyce. 1935—Relations with men. 4. Authors, American—20th century—
Family relationships. 5. Authors, American—20th century—Biography. 6. Jewish
women—United States—Biography. 7. Jewish families—United States. I. Title.
PS3560 O3795Z474 2004
813'.54—dc22
[B]                                                                        2003062133

This book is printed on acid-free paper. ∞

Printed in the United States of America
Set in Adobe Garamond
Designed by Francesca Belanger

*In memory of Peter Pinchbeck*

*&*

*for Judith Dunford,*
*who listened all the way through*

The following of . . . thematic designs through one's life should be, I think, the true purpose of autobiography.

—Vladimir Nabokov, *Speak, Memory*

*Preface*

I once had a husband who started obsessively painting squares—three squares in shifting relationships to each other on what appeared flat ground, colored emptiness. He explained to me that the negative space in his work was as important as the positive, that each took its form from the other. What interested him most was the tension between them. I remember being fascinated by his concept of negative space, though *negative* seemed the wrong word for something that had so much presence.

I was still young then, too young to look at my history and see how my life has shaped itself around absences—first by happenstance; ultimately, perhaps, by choice.

# ONE

# Samuel Rosenberg's Daughters

*Toward the end of her life, when I thought my mother's defenses were finally down, I asked whether she remembered her father's death, which occurred when she was five years old. "Oh, yes," she replied brightly. "He was in a trolley car accident, and we never got the insurance." Then she looked at me with the glimmer of a crafty smile. "You've asked me too late. I've forgotten everything."*

*She had never spoken of what it was like to grow up without a father. In fact, she seemed to lack a recollected girlhood, except for one memory she was willing to call up: the Victory Garden she'd tended during World War I, when her family was living near Bronx Park. Her garden was at the top of a long hill. When she was in her nineties, her mind kept wandering back to that sunlit patch of earth, and she would marvel over and over that the carrots she grew there were the sweetest she'd ever tasted. Otherwise, except for her singing, which had pre-dated my arrival into the world, it was as if my mother's life and memories had begun with me.*

*"I have a trained voice," I'd sometimes hear her tell people. In a bitter way, she seemed proud of that fact. On the music rack of our baby grand was an album of lieder by Schubert, her favorite composer. Once in a while, when one of my aunts induced her to sing, she would*

reluctantly sit down on the piano bench to accompany herself, and her voice would sound to my astonished ears like the performances that issued from the cloth-covered mouth of our wooden radio. Whatever was "classical" was welcomed into our living room, but if you switched to the wrong station and got the blare of a blue note, my mother would give it short shrift. "Popular," as she dismissed all music that was not classical, was "dissonant" and therefore no good, with an exception made for melodies from certain Broadway shows. For months she dusted and cut out her dress patterns humming "My Ship," a song from Kurt Weill's Lady in the Dark. She even decided to teach it to me, though it was really too difficult for a four-year-old. "My ship has sails that are made of silk," I remember singing shyly for my aunts and my father, with my mother prompting, "The decks are trimmed with gold," in her radio mezzo as I faltered.

When I was older, I learned that she had actually been serious about her singing, with ambitions of performing Schubert on the concert stage; at some point, though, she had simply given up. The family didn't want her going on tour, she told me, and besides, there had been no money for further voice training. But perhaps her need and will to sing hadn't been strong enough. I never felt my mother was passionately musical—or passionate about anything except the rarefied, lonely life she envisioned for me with her at my side—effectively shutting out all other relationships—as she guided me toward my destiny of early success.

Her singing may really have been a means to ends other than music itself—a way of setting herself apart as "special," a possible escape route from the blight that had descended upon her sisters. Most of all it may have represented her sole bearable connection to the cultured, artistic father she scarcely remembered, the one thing she had from Samuel Rosenberg in the way of a birthright, which she would pass on to me—not as a gift but as an obligation to be lived out, on her terms.

I was once shown a photograph from another century of a slender, bearded young man. It was right after my grandmother died, when the wall around the past briefly became permeable. "This is your grandfather Samuel," Aunt Anna said, before snatching the picture from my hands as if she just realized she'd committed an indiscretion.

I'd seen a man with bleak, grief-stricken eyes, one hand on an open book as if distractedly keeping his place, the other clenched into a fist. I was sixteen, I had questions. My mother and her older sisters had always told me I was like him—like him in that I'd inherited the talent he had for writing. They'd said he was a poet and a scholar, the descendant of a long line of eminent rabbis in Warsaw. At the age of thirty-seven, he'd died of some illness. That was the story.

I asked my aunt what illness he'd died of. She fell silent, then in a terse, matter-of-fact way let me hear the truth. On April 12, 1908, my grandfather, who had injured his hands in some factory and been out of work for a while, had turned on the gas and killed himself. "Don't tell your mother I told you."

A few days later my mother uncharacteristically took me into her confidence: she and my aunts had found some writings of my grandfather's among my grandmother's papers, and they had burned them. *Burned* them? I remember feeling bereft and estranged, as if something that should have been mine had been stolen from me. "Why did you do that?" I demanded, sure that part of the answer was the suicide my aunt had forbidden me to mention.

My mother seemed startled that I would care so much, that I

would suddenly have such interest in someone I'd never known. "They were private," she said. "They were not for anyone to read."

But poems are written to be read. I knew that at sixteen. I wondered whether she'd lied to me about burning everything. Years later I searched her papers for some yellowed pages with lines in Yiddish or Hebrew, but found nothing in my grandfather's hand.

My mother died with three suitcases still lined up under the piano, exactly where she'd put them in 1984 when she'd moved into her last apartment. In the days when suitcases were called valises, the flaking brown leather one had accompanied my father on business trips to Patchogue or Asbury Park; the blue-and-tan pair had vacationed in the Catskills or in Florida with my mother's older sisters. She, the sole survivor of that generation, had ended up their custodian, as if my father and my aunts had one by one gone off on their holidays, forgetting to bring their luggage.

Although she'd always been house-proud, she didn't seem to

care that the suitcases spoiled the look of her new living room. She needed to go through them slowly, she told me—slowly and with care. "But, Ma, what on earth are you looking for?" I'd ask her. "For something of value," she'd answer cryptically, as if she expected to find a misplaced diamond or stock certificate.

I didn't press her for details. If I probed, I knew she'd pull back altogether or I'd get that glassy smile of hers as she deliberately threw me off track. I was in my fifties now, but since my teens, I'd had difficulty talking to my mother without a filter of ritualized politeness, and I was still careful to reveal only the things about myself that she might find acceptable. Our conversations had little content. I had the feeling that was the way she wanted it. When it came to the adult stranger who was her daughter, she preferred not to deal with too much reality.

A month after her death, I reluctantly spent my first day in her apartment dumping old sweaters, yellowed handkerchiefs, and ancient tea towels into plastic garbage bags. In her desk, I found bundles of old letters and papers and a collection of address books—most had hardly any names written on their pages; a few were completely blank.

Deciding to tackle the suitcases, I dragged them into the middle of the living-room floor. All they'd ever contained were photos, hundreds of them, not only unfamiliar old snapshots of members of my family but studio portraits mounted on heavy cardboard—the kind that used to be shot in storefronts by professionals squinting into one of those big black cameras with accordion fronts.

The decades were as scrambled as the contents of my mother's chests of drawers. You might pull out a sepia portrait of Aunt Anna and Aunt Leona as tiny grave-faced children in Warsaw in the 1890s, followed by a shot of me looking out at the world in surprise from a baby carriage in Brooklyn in 1935; then my mother would appear, attempting to smile in an unbecoming cloche and dress in the flapper era, or in a colored Polaroid from 1960, wearing black on her trip to Israel right after my father died. Perhaps she'd sometimes pored over these pictures with her magnifying glass under the Chinese lamp on the dining table, but there was no sign she'd ever gone through them with the intention of labeling them or creating order. I had the feeling she'd left it to me to make what sense of them I could. Maybe she'd never looked at them at all, kept putting it off until her memory went and what might have troubled her once didn't matter anymore. "I have a very good forgettery," she had taken to saying with eerie satisfaction.

I was not surprised when my grandfather turned up forty-five years after I'd last seen him—immediately I recognized the portrait Aunt Anna had put out of sight. Then I was excited to come upon an ethereal old man in a black robe and a yarmulke, who unmistakably resembled him. The old man's finely drawn features were framed by earlocks and a long white beard. The photographer, someone named R. Majorkiewczl, had posed the two of them—they were clearly father and son—the same way, perhaps on the same afternoon one hundred and ten years ago, shortly before my grandfather Samuel Rosenberg sailed for America with his wife and two small daughters. In each photo was the same open book, the same bamboo stand. My great-grandfather, a reflective, spiritual-looking person, perhaps more resigned to the coming separation than his son, appeared to be looking inward, not outward . . . I'll never know his name. There's no one alive who remembers it.

My grandmother Eva Rosenberg believed in the Evil Eye. For luck, she'd bury a smooth white stone at the bottom of a crock of sauerkraut. Several years older than her husband, she was a shopkeeper's daughter just educated enough to be able to read a Yiddish newspaper. My grandfather must have been no more than sixteen or seventeen when their marriage was arranged—a union of opposites. Aunt Anna once said they'd had little in common.

When my grandparents landed in America, they would soon find that the intellectual achievements that had made my grandfather seem a promising young man in Warsaw had no negotiable value. In one factory after another in the grim cast-iron loft buildings of downtown New York, the mistakes made by my grandfather's clumsy, shaking hands would lead to his downfall. Within a few years he had more children to support with the hateful jobs he had such difficulty keeping. A frail asthmatic boy named Uda was born in 1899, and in 1903, my mother (her fourteen-year-old sister Anna, who loved Shakespeare, insisted they call her Rosalind).

In the earliest photo of my mother, she's a bright-eyed four-year-old, wearing high-buttoned shoes, a short heavy linen dress with perfectly ironed pleats, and a big white bow in her flaxen hair. She's holding a nosegay and smiling—fully smiling—there's nothing forced about it. She's the adored youngest child, a bright spot in the lives of her anxious family, not at all intimidated by her visit to the photographer's studio.

By the next photo, taken three or four years later, that particular smile has vanished. In the interim came my grandfather's angry exit from a world in which he could not find his bearings. My mother's smile evidently never reappeared.

The family was precariously kept from destitution by Anna and Leona, who even while their father was alive had needed to find jobs right after high school, and by the continued largesse of a relative of my grandmother's, who had helped them establish themselves in America. Aunt Marcia had left Warsaw in the 1850s and made an advantageous marriage to a wealthy widower in the

United States. She enjoyed to the full her power over her poor relations. Her humiliating interference in my grandfather's household had undoubtably contributed to his misery.

In November 1908, six months after Samuel Rosenberg's death, Aunt Marcia was away from New York, visiting in-laws in Shreveport. A postcard she sent to my grandmother indicates that she had taken my mother along with her. Was Eva Rosenberg still too distraught to take care of her youngest child? Was my mother unable to forget something she had seen the day her father turned on the gas?

Aunt Marcia's message, signed "Much love," has a peremptory tone: "Took the child out shopping. Never mind if she misses school a day. I want her ready."

On the other side of the card is a disturbing photo of three women dressed in black, as if for a funeral. My grandmother is in the middle, looking dazed and numb under the weight of a hat loaded with black feathers, with the hawk-faced Aunt Marcia's hand on her shoulder.

Perhaps Aunt Marcia wished to remind the niece who had lost her husband in such a disgraceful way of the gratitude she expected for continuing to support her and the four orphans. Under the photo is the incongruously cheerful inscription: "Here is a picture of the three home folks." Beneath this are the wavering capital letters of a little girl just learning to write.

On that postcard I found an unexpected address: 428 East 120th Street. I didn't know my mother and her family had ever lived in East Harlem, a neighborhood whose brownstones and tenements were filled with Eastern European Jews at the turn of the century. I can imagine how relieved they must have felt when they were finally able to escape from the tainted rooms where my grandfather had taken his own life to the fresh air of the Bronx.

They not only changed their address, they cast off the name my grandfather had given them. In 1919, my grandmother and her four children petitioned the City Court of New York to let them become the Rosses. I'd never heard about that either, though each year on April 12, the Ross family lit a *yahrzeit* candle for Samuel Benjamin Rosenberg.

Like my mother, I would seek ways of resurrecting him. But the paths I took were different. I'd search for Samuel Rosenberg in exiles, in artists who could not find acceptance, in the rage and sadness of these men that would make me fall in love with them and ultimately leave me alone again with my freedom.

I'm looking at a snapshot of Anna and Leona away on vacation in one of those resort camps where young white-collar workers began vacationing in the 1920s. On a rustic porch around twilight, the two unmarried sisters lean back in Adirondack chairs, bored and pensive in limp cotton dresses; a third woman broods in the shadows. The three of them, all in their early thirties, seem unconsoled by each others' company. The picture was taken during one of those crucial two-week hiatuses from ordinary life when a stenographer or bookkeeper was given license to feel free, when there was even the possibility of life-changing encounters. But nothing has happened yet, and nothing will.

A Chekhovian stillness in the midst of the Jazz Age.

For a few years the family believed that my mother's luck would be very different from her sisters'. She was not only considerably younger but the one who had been born in America, the one with blond hair, blue eyes, and a delicate, sweet-faced prettiness for which she got a lot of attention. She had the kind of refined air that went well with her new American name and might lead to an excellent marriage. Aunt Marcia, who had always taken particular interest in Rosalind, offered to pay for voice lessons once she finished high school, though Anna and Leona would have to continue to support her. Anna was willing to make sacrifices; Leona couldn't help feeling resentful. Aunt Marcia seemed to have delegated Rosalind to live for all of them.

By the 1920s, Aunt Marcia was in her eighties, but she still had the energy of an irresistible life force, an intensity that made my mother and her sisters feel washed out in comparison, as if the old woman were feeding on their hunger, their youth.

Leona, who believed she had inherited Samuel Rosenberg's literary aspirations, once set out to write a sentimental portrait of "Auntie" in the flowery language of the quotations she copied into her commonplace book. "My great-aunt Marcia," she began, "is a very old lady of unusual personality, retaining suggestions of former great beauty. Her hair is white, soft and fluffy as a fresh snowfall. Her wit and wisdom have only been sharpened by time."

After a few more trite observations of this sort, Leona allowed herself a moment of harsher judgment: "Life has been good to my Great-Aunt Marcia, endowing her with money and the opportunity to see the world, a husband who adored her and was in turn adored. The world has catered to her as to a queen, and to this day she still retains her little court, but this has made her imperious and unbending."

To the fatherless three sisters, whose social life was practically nonexistent, Aunt Marcia seemed dazzlingly well connected, her sphere of influence extending south and west; Auntie even seemed to know people in New York's artistic circles. One acquaintance, Mme Anna Ziegler, was a former Metropolitan Opera singer who had established the Ziegler Academy of Normal Singing in the Hotel Wellington, a stone's throw from Carnegie Hall. She was enlisted by Aunt Marcia to train my mother's voice.

Mme Ziegler seemed impressed by the diligence of her seventeen-year-old student. In response to a note from Aunt Marcia in 1920,

requesting a progress report and enclosing a check, Mme Ziegler wrote, "I can only say that the latter is doing as well as any student ever could do in the same time. As a matter of fact she is just finishing the work allotted to the second year of training." But the element of excitement seemed to be missing from Mme Ziegler's gracious words.

My mother had recently made her debut in a student recital at the Bowery Mission, singing "Last Night a Nightingale Woke Me."

Mme Ziegler's musicales, held in various halls around the city, were as close as my mother ever came to appearing on the concert stage.

While my mother dreamed of Carnegie Hall, other girls she met at Mme Ziegler's were auditioning for the musicals and revues proliferating on Broadway. In the summer of 1921, a fellow student, George Marsh, encouraged her to do likewise, sending her a list of managers and agents. She shared the list with Edna Robinson, a young woman who lived on her own at the Parnassus Club and who was calling upon three managers a day even in the midst of an August heat wave. But my mother did not seem motivated to try her luck. She even found it hard to write to a manager in Pittsburgh Mme Ziegler herself had suggested. Perhaps fear of being subjected to the "crudities" other girls whispered about held her back, or her proud disdain for popular music, or profound uncertainty about her actual talent.

That fall Auntie Marcia interrupted the voice training. She had changed her mind about my mother's future and had now decided to send her out into the world to attract a suitable fiancé as soon as possible. She bought train tickets for her protégée to Vancouver, Shreveport, Dallas—all cities where prosperous relatives of her late husband's would see that the pretty little thing met the right people. Not that the musical training would go to waste. Auntie had the quaint Victorian notion that my mother's singing constituted sort of a finishing touch—it was the accomplishment of a cultured girl and would give her an effective way of standing out at social gatherings, when young people clustered around the piano to hear a little Schubert. The eighty-year-old woman was unaware of the advent of the Charleston and the Bunny Hop or of the flasks of gin men who had fought in the war were carrying in their jacket pockets.

World War I had jolted young people into the Roaring Twenties, but my mother and her sisters still existed as though time had stopped when my grandfather died. Anna and Leona had been abruptly deprived of their youth, burdened immediately with the duty of devoting themselves to my grandmother in place of the husband who had abandoned her in a strange country. Neither of "the girls," as my aunts were called even when their hair turned gray, was ever supposed to leave home. The wages they turned over each week earned them no freedom. For most of her adult life, Anna shared a bedroom with her mother. Leona, who was considered "selfish," escaped to the golf course or the tennis courts on weekends and occasionally demanded to entertain her friends. My grandmother, still ashamed of her husband's suicide and fearful of losing control over her daughters, wanted no one to cross her threshold who was not a member of the family.

"Nettie wanted to visit me some evening," Leona complained in a letter to Rosalind in November 1921, shortly after her arrival in Vancouver, "but of course Ma put her foot down and I had to make an excuse. If you can't have privileges at home, I wonder where you can expect them."

On the other side of the continent, my shy mother, plunged into a social whirl for the first time in her life, was trying to keep her head above water. "Rosalind seems to be enjoying herself," Aunt Marcia's niece Frankie reported to Auntie in December, "hardly has time to catch her breath between goes. She is out with Sol Meyer tonight, his first date—she has not been rushed as yet, but really has not met all the boys."

The predicted rush evidently never came, although my mother was shown off in various outfits at luncheons and parties. "Wore her pink dress at Retta's Sunday and certainly looked beautiful," Frankie wrote. But between the lines there seemed to be a problem, something Frankie couldn't quite articulate, something— some lack of vivacity or confidence—that kept my mother from rising fully to the occasion. "I would like her to know how to play bridge before she goes to Dallas," Frankie told Aunt Marcia. "She is anxious to learn, but that takes time." She seemed to be saying her young visitor needed lessons in how to be light-hearted.

"I suppose you are quite a card shark by now," my mother's brother Uda wrote her on January 8, 1922, "and have won all sorts of useless prizes. You must try to cultivate a southern drawl while you are down there as it will make quite a hit in N.Y."

My mother, who was in Shreveport by then—nervously sewing up a couple of new dresses in preparation for being launched in Dallas—had evidently grown more accustomed to bridge parties, even if she did not really enjoy them. Perhaps they reminded her that she could only pretend to fit in, although she kept such feelings to herself. In her later life she adamantly refused to play bridge.

During the remainder of my mother's trip, Uda was too busy to correspond. He had served as a navy radioman during the war; now in every spare minute he was broadcasting from his own ham radio station in the basement, which had just been picked up in France and Alberta, Canada. But Anna and Leona wrote every few days. They wrote even though they had essentially nothing to report.

"Dear Rosalind," typed Leona, stealing a few minutes from the two lawyers she worked for, "I haven't anything new to tell you. Everything about the same, except the weather, which varies constantly. It is snowing steadily now and is grey and dismal out. It seems more and more difficult to get up mornings.

"If you continue getting more clothes, Rosalind," Leona continued, "the problem will arise of where to put them, and you will need another trunk to get home. Frankie is indeed a fairy godmother, and you are the fairy princess. Sometimes fairy tales do come true!!!

"Glad you got the invitation to Little Rock. You should certainly go, by all means. If I had a magic carpet, I'd go to the ends of the earth."

Just before my mother began her voice training at Mme Ziegler's, Aunt Marcia had bought my grandmother a small house in Brooklyn within walking distance of her much more lavish one and had moved the whole family out there, so that she could be closer to "her court." The new neighborhood, Mapleton, which adjoined Borough Park, was a sparsely populated enclave of modest brick homes with wooden porches, surrounded by acres of empty lots where other nondescript houses and stores were just beginning to be built. The unpaved streets, dusty in summer, muddy in winter, led to some working farms where eggs could be purchased.

But Mapleton's rural qualities did not charm Auntie's great-nieces. When they came home from their jobs and walked down the steps of the Elevated station, they found themselves in a small town in the middle of nowhere. For unescorted culture-hungry women of slender means, nighttime Manhattan, with its theaters and concert halls and liveliness, was both a subway ride and an infinity away—a focus of longings impossible to fulfill. As Leona disgustedly put it, knowing her little sister would agree with her, "Brooklyn is a state of being (dead) and New York is a state of pocket."

Leona had no women friends in Mapleton—they had been left behind in the far reaches of the Bronx. The neighbors seemed too coarse to bother talking to. For male companionship, she and Anna had to rely upon their younger brother and an annoying cousin named Herman, who apparently had a crush on my mother and who far too frequently called upon the sisters during her absence. There was also a dog named Judge, whose exploits, in lieu of other news, filled Leona's letters; she relished describing his unruly masculine behavior—how he roamed the area, consorting with others of his species, blackening his white coat.

"You are not missing much in Mapleton. It is as dull as a cemetery," Anna wrote one Sunday. "We are in the kitchen eating Charlotte Russes—our new indulgence. Herman did not come today. I wonder why." Despite a wry tone that occasionally surfaced, Anna, unlike Leona, never expressed a longing to escape from her duties, never used an expression like "fairy princess" that might make her little sister feel guilty about enjoying herself, though she did wish Rosalind would write home more than once a week and go into much more detail.

But my mother may have felt that she too had little of any real consequence to report. She had seen a lot of the continent through dusty train windows, had been taken to Hollywood and Yellowstone Park as well as innumerable parties where her home-sewn dresses looked distinctly dowdy compared to the chiffons and georgettes of southern belles and where boys who clearly weren't Jewish had looked her over and asked her to do the two-step. On those grounds she could keep assuring everyone she was having a wonderful time, but she must have been uneasily aware that most of her enjoyment was coming from the sheer novelty of the trip. The truth was, she had absolutely nothing to show for it—no name of a potential suitor, let alone an engagement ring—when she returned to Mapleton in April.

My mother came back in time to graduate from the Ziegler Academy of Normal Singing with a rendition of "None but the Lonely Heart" at the last musicale of the season. Shortly afterward she received an affectionate but worried note from Mme Ziegler: "Rosalind dear, I am thinking much over your future. Please, dear, realize that you must become expressive and lively in order to fill engagements."

By 1922 Aunt Marcia was ailing, although she hated to acknowledge that her own traveling days were over. "I feel like a cripple," she would say impatiently to her great-nieces, "when I want to move about and go here and there." But she still had her money, so her ability to fiddle with lives was unimpaired. For Anna, who would soon be middle-aged and would always be needed at home, she could, of course, do nothing, but Leona's misery and outbursts of temper could not be ignored. "Aunt knows someone in Pittsburgh and is trying to ship me there," Leona told Rosalind that winter. Uda was commanded by Aunt Marcia to stop wasting his time on radio, an invention that would never come to anything, and look around for a store where he could start his own business and where Rosalind could assist him eventually—but not immediately.

Although she had turned nineteen in February, my mother's time had not quite run out. Aunt Marcia sent her back to Mme Ziegler's to further develop her poise and her repertoire and consulted with Frankie. In late November, Rosalind was dispatched to Shreveport, where she was to be given another chance.

By now my mother was more experienced and knew what to expect. Just before she left, she'd even had enough faith in her future prospects to fend off a boring young Borough Park doctor who had become infatuated with her, though she made the mistake of giving him her Shreveport address.

"No wonder people think you were born with a gold spoon in your mouth," the note he wrote her early in January began, followed by some fatuous remarks about the contrasting climates of

New York and Louisiana: "While we are suffering the extreme cold with constant snow storms here, you are enjoying summer, green leaves, grass, and hot sunshine," etc., etc. Then came a barrage of proprietary questions: "Please let me know how long you are there, how do you pass your time, how do you like the place and how long do you intend to stay there."

My mother sent the note up to Anna for analysis. "I do think you should answer it," Anna wrote back on January 26 from her desk at the Conay Glove Company. "Kill him with kindness, that's the best method. After all he treated you as well as he possibly knows how and you treated him rather shabbily at the end. Of course it does not make any material difference, but it pays to be polite. So much for the Doc."

As usual when writing about any of the useless men in their lives, Anna adopted a withering tone. She had run into "the Doc" in Manhattan at a lecture where he was "the big I AM." Afterward there was dancing, "but I did not stay because I had Herman with me. Would have had a nicer time if I had gone alone."

She was enclosing twenty-five dollars so that Rosalind could buy herself a hat the minute she reached Dallas. And there were other needed items on their way: stockings, two pairs of white kid gloves, and an instruction book for the mandolin. "Enjoy yourself all you can," Anna wrote, "while you are in the swim. Don't worry about what you will do later. The future will take care of itself." She seemed to know how driven Rosalind must feel under the weight of everyone's expectations, how badly she needed permission to just take life as it came.

My mother had come back from her first trip full of questions about the ennui and isolation of her sisters; by now she was desperately anxious to find some permanent means of escape. One thing she had learned out in the world to her pain was how much depended upon having the right appearance. Moving among a free-spending crowd, competing with doctors' daughters and stylish Dallas girls whose fathers had made fortunes with oil wells, she had often felt humiliated by the wardrobe that marked her as a poor relation, even when she reminded herself that she was just as pretty as anyone and a lot more talented. This time she had appealed to Anna, though she must have felt terrible about doing so. But Rosalind had no one she felt closer to. Anna had always been more like a mother than a sister.

Writing to Rosalind during the winter months of 1923, Anna never complains about the five- or ten-dollar postal orders extracted from her own spending money that she encloses with each letter. For her little sister, she scours the bargain racks of the Brooklyn department stores with a sense of mission. "Am I keeping you supplied?" she asks gaily, having just put into the mail a pair of jersey knickers for Rosalind to wear on a camping holiday with some of her new acquaintances.

On this second trip, my mother knew it was now or never for her to find the man of refinement who would recognize her specialness. Animated by the urgency she felt, perhaps she almost flowered. A reticent letter writer compared to her sisters, she tended to conceal her feelings in stilted language. But for a month or two she evidently became eloquent. "I hope there will be a letter from you when I get home tonight," Leona wrote. "for that is our latest diversion, and we are delighted that you are enjoying everything to the utmost. In fact, it is as if we had the same experience. Auntie is pleased beyond all measure. Every time a letter arrives, we have several sessions, one with the family, another with Auntie, and we discuss the pros and cons of the situation."

The experiences Rosalind let them share vicariously seemed to energize the sisters. Leona was able to envision a trip out west with her friend Elizabeth: "We are going to sling our knapsacks on our backs and scour the U.S. for adventure. Ma is willing, and Auntie urges it. It all depends upon finances." Leona also announced that she and Anna had started going out "two or three times during the week. I guess it is rather hard on Ma, but we would be bored if we didn't have any activities."

Leona was taking mandolin lessons herself and going to the Rand School for a night course in creative writing, where her sentimental effusions were getting C's; she made Uda buy a suit and escort her to the Rand School dance. Anna was attending a series of lectures by Dr. Oliver Wendell Holmes on Shakespeare's tragedies. "Herman was there too," she wrote in mid-February, just before Rosalind's departure for Dallas. "He follows me up like a Burns detective. He has had entirely too much of my time and I am going to shake him for good. He is far from being that innocent little creature that he pretends to be. I don't want you to go around with him when you come home."

In Dallas, as the remaining weeks rushed by, my mother went on a round of parties that never stopped and even gave an impromptu singing recital at one of them. But the names of young men—Arnie, Dudley, Gus, Aaron—that flashed by in the unfolding serial of her "36-hour days" had the vanishing habits of shooting stars. Some of her admirers were evidently not Jewish. For a while the name Jimmy Ferguson seemed to have some staying power until he took my mother to a picnic where a Texas siren shamelessly lured him away.

Leona, who knew little about the ways of men, had a fine time waxing indignant: "You can put it under the heading of experience. Some girls are treacherous. I don't think a man would have acted so contemptible and small. Well, you have them on the list & they never will be missed!"

But it was the kind of news that probably made Anna feel heartsick, because Rosalind was really almost out of time. Unless she had extraordinary luck, it seemed inevitable that very soon she would be back in Mapleton for good. They couldn't afford to keep her afloat in the world much longer.

Although she was still sending home the letters that kept Leona and Aunt Marcia so entertained, my mother herself was growing worried. In March, short of pocket money and of fashionable outfits for the changing weather, she wrote to Anna offering to return immediately, though she did have an invitation to stay on in Dallas a few weeks longer.

"Stay there as long as possible," Anna replied immediately. "Send me a telegram and let me know how much you need. You could not get this opportunity again and therefore I want you to make the most of it. It is foolish to trifle about another few dollars." But as she typed the next two lines her own despair overwhelmed her: "There is absolutely no chance to make any worthwhile friends up here. We never meet anyone from one year to the other and those that we do meet are not worth anything."

For three more weeks my mother hung on in Dallas. "When do you expect to be home, Rosalind?" Leona wrote. "I suppose you will be home by Passover. You surely can't miss the matzos. Auntie told me the other night, totally uncalled for, that I would have plenty to wear when you got home."

My mother left Texas at the end of March, unable to say good-bye in person to each one of the new friends she'd made. She called her condition "the grippe," but it could have been depression—a sense of terrible anticlimax.

Recovering in Mapleton on April 8, she spent the day methodically writing thank-you notes to a list of twenty-two people in Dallas she never expected to set eyes on again, eight of whom were young men. The words to express the appropriate, conventional sentiments did not come easily. Among my mother's papers, I found a few listless drafts begun on blue stationery, only to be abandoned in mid-sentence. "I wish to thank you for that perfectly lovely dinner, which I enjoyed so much . . . I shall never forget the delightful time I had in Dallas. . . . It is getting warmer now and we shall soon have spring. . . . Hoping I may have the pleasure of meeting you again."

During the eight mysterious weeks she spent in Dallas, my mother may have fallen for one of the men on her mailing list. There were two attempts to write to someone called Fred. The first breaks off in the midst of an apology for having been too overwhelmed by the grippe to see him. In the second, my mother swiftly moves to a less personal topic—her hope that Fred's mother is "her sunny self once again"—before making a brave effort to sound blithe about being home: "New York is so rushing, such a contrast to Dallas—can hardly realize that I am only back a week. Saw the 'Chauve Souris' and 'Rain,' which is considered the finest play of the season."

Her next sentence, the last one before she stops herself from going on, may have seemed a bit too revealing.

"The spring isn't here yet," my mother writes as if suddenly the weather up north is no longer promising, "and I am very restless."

There is a coda to this story: A note from an officer of the Texas National Guard, dated June 17, 1923, addressed to Miss Rosalind Ross in care of the Majestic Theater in Dallas, apologizing for having to break a date—a piece of evidence that my mother had briefly returned to Texas without any help from Aunt Marcia and possibly without her family's approval. She was on the road, in the chorus of *Rosemarie,* an operetta touring the state.

A dozen snapshots show my mother thoroughly enjoying being

on her own. She had quickly found the kind of ebullient best friend she'd always needed, a stunning adventurous young woman named Caroline Robinson. They posed together laughing, arm in arm, dressed up in flowery Japanese kimonos. Soon two young men (was one of them Fred?) were taking them around. In one shot, the foursome are visiting a ranch where my mother has been induced to perform a tentative arabesque atop a gatepost; in another, my mother is powdering her nose in front of a Mexican cantina after they've all crossed the border in a dust-caked Ford. Her escort is handsome and attentive and very blond. He sits so close to her that his suntanned arm brushes against hers—she doesn't dare look at him. She takes a photo of him astride a dark horse back with her to Mapleton.

She couldn't stay out there forever. It was over before September, all of it—her show-business escapade, the long train trips south, the voice lessons, the chances. The girl who ran off to sing in Texas was not the mother I knew.

The summer before I started college, I spent my weekday mornings at the Therese M. Aub Secretarial School at 108th and Broadway. I was fifteen years old. Therese M. Aub was a stooped-over ancient lady with a clubfoot and yellow-white hair screwed up tightly in a bun. She would clomp up and down between the tables, looking at her watch as the typewriters clicked at different speeds and a brass-bladed fan, circa 1932, sporadically rattled sheets of paper and you tried to rev up toward the championship goal of typing "The quick brown fox jumped over the lazy dog" at 120 wpm. Time passed like very old slow time from another era.

At eleven your fingers got a vacation from the stiff keys of the tall black machine, and you crossed your legs and put a steno pad on your knee as Miss Aub dictated, "Thanking you for yours of the eighteenth. I am sorry to say the shipment of the ninth has so far failed to arrived," giving you a preview of what you might have to listen to for the rest of your life.

Release came at noon. I'd rush down the stairs and hit the street where it was still 1951, strangely dazed, as if part of my mind had been put to sleep. If I had a dollar, I'd head for Washington

Square Park, where my bohemian friends hung out, or the Thalia movie theater, where each day they had a new double bill of French films like *Devil in the Flesh* or *Un Chien Andalou.* If I had to go home, my mother would be waiting with her coiled-up anxiety. "How did it go?"

She had sent me to Therese M. Aub, as she had been sent by Auntie years before I came into the picture. Therese M. Aub prepared you for what you would do if you failed.

"I hope, Rosalind," Leona had written my mother from her office desk at 129 Broadway one Saturday in March 1923, "that it will never be your lot to have to do stenography. It is the most uninspiring work, sickening for women. On a glorious Saturday afternoon, when almost the whole world is at leisure, I feel virtually like a prisoner up in a tower, incarcerated until the sun sets, but it doesn't do to rail at high heaven."

My mother accepted her stenographic destiny, since there were no other options, although she did correspond with one of her voice teachers and sang from time to time herself on a small radio station, heard in Newark, that Uda started with some of his friends. She settled down to a job in an advertising agency, where she was so highly thought of by her gentlemanly boss that he presented her with a portrait of an Italian peasant girl in a red head scarf, painted on a small wooden panel, which he had brought back from his European travels.

The portrait was supposed to be a valuable piece of art. What its exact value was, no one knew, though it was very dark and old enough to be slightly cracked down the center. It would later hang in our living room in a place of honor just above the George Steck baby grand my mother purchased with most of her savings a few months after she married my father. A Steck, she always insisted, was almost as good as a Steinway.

Caroline Robinson, who was still touring, kept in touch with my mother for a while after she gave up on her singing career. Breathless accounts of various on-the-road misadventures, scrawled on the stationery of small-town hotels, would arrive in the mail. In September 1923, Caroline was in Brownwood, Texas, having a miserable time in the chorus of *Irene.* The trouble was, the other single young women were of the "chorus-type, so ordinary and coarse we have nothing in common. Their conversations backstage are so vulgar and degrading. You were very lucky in your first show to be with a really superior class of girls." She was going to stick it out a few months longer, but vowed, "This is my last year of the stage."

If my mother was still secretly tempted to try out for more operettas, what Caroline wrote may have put an end to such ideas. Here was everything Aunt Marcia and her sisters had warned her about—the awfulness that could envelop you and make you shopworn and cheap. All my mother had left was her proud feeling of superior refinement.

The following spring Caroline, who was now teaching ballet to little girls in Palm Beach Springs, popped up in New York. My mother's boss was so taken with the spirited young woman that he wrote her an admiring note after she visited the office. A year later, Caroline was off to Paris; on a new liner named for the ill-fated *Lusitania,* she had an ecstatic romance with a wealthy and handsome young British doctor, who wined, dined, and probably seduced her in first class, but unfortunately turned out to be married when they disembarked. "Oh Rosalind, Rosalind, you can't imagine the pain!" My mother could imagine it all too well. Here was another cautionary tale about the sexual perils of independence.

* * *

There are no photos of my mother taking her bobbed hair out of curlers in the bedroom she shared with Leona, no shots of her presenting her boss with a folder of impeccably typed business letters or taking the BMT back to Mapleton in the summer heat or ironing a dress in my grandmother's kitchen to wear at work the following day. People in the 1920s were camera-crazy, but usually didn't find the daily routine worth recording. The old brownish pictures of my mother and her sisters give the impression that they spent their lives on vacation.

Leona, throwing herself into amateur theatricals, shrieks with laughter as a Keystone Kop raises his hand to spank her in her flounced baby costume. On a mountain hike, in plus fours and feathered alpine hat, she communes with a blue jay perched on her wrist. Demurely, my mother, all in white like Daisy in *The Great Gatsby,* waves at an unseen photographer from the seat of a dog cart. In a more candid shot, she's captured on a boat ride, shrinking politely away with closed eyes from the embrace of a fellow with a dark mustache and thick round eyeglasses who seems too old for her. Anna always looks unaccustomed to leisure. Surrounded by Leona and other reclining bathers in tank suits, she sits straight up on the sands of a beach, surreally dressed from head to foot for a day at the office; in a row of merry campers perched on a log at Camp Copake, she can't quite produce the carefree look expected of her.

Frequently the three sisters pose together, unable to separate even away from Mapleton. Only the old-fashioned outfits keep changing significantly, and the generic scenery—here a lake, there a porch, field, or fence. The weather remains stationary—always sunny.

The fashions of the flapper decade do not seem right for my mother. For waistless dresses, she is too small and full-breasted;

knickers and long socks foreshorten her legs; tank suits sag around her hips; she lacks the requisite insouciance for cloche hats, which only seem to extinguish her. By twenty-one her delicate bloom has markedly begun to fade, and she would prefer not to be photographed at all. "Don't look at me," she seems to be saying. "I am

not what you think. I would much rather be elsewhere." She will never again be as lovely as in one lakeside photo taken around 1918, where she looks like a Pre-Raphaelite wood nymph with her head thrown back, her long thick hair flying about. When I found that picture, at first I did not recognize her.

In 1919, after she almost died in the Spanish flu epidemic, her hair thinned so much that she had to wear it short in the new postwar style. Perhaps she felt diminished when she recovered, no longer certain of her beauty, which she would soon need so badly when Aunt Marcia sent her out into the world. As she grew older, her beauty may have seemed like so many things in her life—an unkept promise.

The camp photos show a series of admirers to whom my
mother seems to deny connection. Even when they put their arms
around her waist, she doesn't appear to know them. There is one
blond handsome bull of a man with sardonic Slavic features who
crops up repeatedly in the group shots she saved one summer,
though it's hard to tell whether he's interested in my mother or
Leona. He looks like a potential source of grief for one of them,
an overbearing fellow used to having his way with women. He
comes to a party in Mapleton—one of the rare times the sisters
entertained—where he glowers mockingly in the background
while my mother stares forbearingly at the camera.

Then he is gone, replaced by my father. By now, it's the summer of 1929.

According to family legend, it was my mother's trained voice that
first attracted my father's attention. Still a bachelor at thirty-four,
my father, Daniel Glassman, was standing on the shore of Lake
Copake when he was surprised by a burst of mezzo-soprano
singing from across the water, where a solitary young woman was
plying the oars of a rowboat among the lily pads as she swayed
gracefully back and forth. My father was captivated by the free
concert and the lovely singer, so alluringly out of reach. Whether
he jumped into a rowboat to pursue her or waited for her to row
back to land, he soon found a way to introduce himself.

My mother in turn was struck by my father's British accent, so
different from the New York Jewish inflections of other men at the
camp. Here was someone cultured and gentlemanly. She had
nearly given up on finding a "gentleman"—a Jewish fellow who
didn't *seem* Jewish.

In those days my father was cute—with a round, schoolboyish
face, straight brown hair that flopped endearingly over his right

eye, and a trim physique, which he would quickly lose to my mother's cooking. He was short, but she was shorter. Right from the start they looked like a pair. People would often remark that the two of them could be taken for brother and sister. My father had a sense of humor, good manners, a hopeful outlook, and a nonthreatening amiability that my mother responded to immediately. He was unfamiliar with Schubert but at least loved Gilbert and Sullivan.

"Your father never raised his voice," my mother used to say, as if that had been his outstanding quality. She may have had shadowy memories of Samuel Rosenberg's dark moods, of her parents shouting at each other in the tenement in East Harlem.

In Mapleton voices were raised a great deal, with Leona constantly stirring up trouble in the household and my mother often called upon to act as mediator. Her sisters' fights even ruined her vacations. Perhaps she had taken off in the rowboat to get away from them the day she met my father.

Very quickly they seem to have had the beginnings of an understanding, though for a while my father was in the dark about where he stood. At Camp Copake, my mother may have had a certain reputation—unapproachable, hard to please, a pretty girl with a disdainful attitude toward the high jinks of the other campers.

Wearying of Copake soon after they met, my mother threw my father into confusion by suddenly going off to a new camp, Arcady, alone, just before he returned to work in the city. But then a note from her arrived, suggesting he come up for a weekend. He tried very hard to sound offhanded when he wrote back on August 10: "Dear Rosalind, Your glowing description of Arcady just swept me off my feet. I know that you are not addicted to the use of negatives, so it would seem that so far your vacation has not been particularly successful."

Having taken pains to disguise his happiness that my mother was not enjoying herself without him, my father devoted a few lines to the weather conditions in New York, very warm but "better than it has been all week . . . maybe the weatherman has decided to relent so that next week and most assuredly the weekend (selfish mortal that I am) will be perfect. I am sure," he wrote, in a burst of tremendous confidence, "that by the time I see you, you will be in an entirely different mood."

But as he ended his letter, my father clearly could not quite believe his luck: "Should you decide to go to some other place next Saturday, try and arrange not to leave until the afternoon.

"Feeling great and trust you are the same," he concluded, losing control of his syntax. "Sincerely, Dan."

Daniel Glassman began courting Rosalind Ross just as the Great Depression cast its pall over American life. Once, hoping to wow her, he took her to a Fifth Avenue hotel for lunch. He blanched when he caught sight of the prices on the menu, but did not have the nerve to suggest they immediately walk out. With one look, my mother realized that he could not afford the meal. "I'll have graham crackers and milk," she quickly said to the waiter. My father, no doubt embarrassed by her face-saving choice but immensely grateful, did not protest as he should have. A bowl of sodden crackers was brought to the table, surrounded by cracked ice in a silver tureen. "It's my favorite dish," my mother insisted like an O. Henry heroine, with what I imagine was that self-sacrificing look of smiling through tears that would begin to crop up in snapshots and would eventually become her characteristic expression.

My parents fared much better during the Depression than the millions of people who actually became destitute. For one thing, they'd had little enough to lose. For another, they managed to keep working. It was true that the ad agency that had employed my mother for six years went out of business right after the Crash, but she did find another position in the stock transfer department of a railway company, though for ten dollars less a week—she would never work her way back up to the fifty-dollar heights of her first job or find herself in such congenial surroundings. Her next employer, a nose, ear, and throat specialist, was able to offer her thirty-five until he abruptly had to reduce his workforce. In her last position, she took dictation from the unpleasant vice president of a wallpaper company, where she was terrified of being fired if they discovered she was married.

She must have consoled herself with the thought that she wouldn't have to work forever, and she counted on my father to make a success of himself once times got better. But even when they did in the next decade, my father stubbornly clung to his low-paying bookkeeping and auditing job—the one he'd been offered in 1921, right after he'd landed in America with two letters of reference from his London employers. He worked for the Metropolitan Tobacco Company, a distributor of cigars and cigarettes, until he died, after a botched operation for ulcers, at sixty-two. Although the company had cut his salary right after I was born, they'd stayed in business— Americans kept smoking straight through the Depression.

My father had left England with his mother, his sister Rose, and his younger brother Henry after two deaths in his family. On the last day of the war, hours before the Armistice, his older brother Abe had been killed in France; when the news reached England, my paternal grandfather had a fatal heart attack. The Glassmans had crossed the ocean, looking for a fresh start.

They didn't talk much about Abe, but they kept the photos and greeting cards he'd sent home from the front, and Aunt Rose, years later, visited his grave in France shortly before her own death. My father had grown up in the reflected glory of Abe's vitality—Abe had been the star, the bright hope of the family. I can even see this, I think, in his lean, clever, vibrant face, which bears an odd resemblance to my son's. In the midst of war he looks fearless and young, happy in the company of the men around him, always ready for another good laugh. He poses jauntily with a shovel, his soldier's cap tilted to one side. "See where your darling lies sleeping," he jokes at the bottom of a photo taken in the trenches. He was obviously planning on staying very much alive. By some miracle, he survived four years of fighting until one of the last shots fired caught up with him.

Perhaps my mother should have married someone as dashing as Abe, someone who would have challenged her, laughed away her pretensions and fears, taught her to embrace a more earthly reality. Instead she chose an adoring, compliant man accustomed to the role of second fiddle. My father had idolized his older brother. In the new family he was starting, he was content to let my mother be the star. She never forgave him for giving her exactly what she thought she wanted.

They got married at the start of their two-week vacations on August 16, 1931. My mother wore a long, bias-cut, cream-colored lace dress she had made herself, one of her most becoming creations, with a corsage of gardenias pinned against her shoulder. For their honeymoon they went to a hotel in Lake George. There someone photographed them sitting in the midst of a field dotted with daisies—my mother in a white summer dress with the sun in her eyes, my father proudly holding her hand. She looks almost happy in a tremulous way, like an exhausted runner glad for the moment to come to rest.

Their marriage, the outcome of a placid two-year engagement, had been somewhat upstaged by Anna's astonishing elopement. On July 31 she had run off to Stamford, Connecticut, to become the wife of a fellow she had known only a short time—a recent émigré from Russia, who worked as a printer and had been a de-

vout follower of Leon Trotsky. Like my father, he had a name with glass in it: Roman Blueglass.

Because Anna and Roman had eloped, there were no wedding photos. Or more likely there were some that later got ripped into little pieces and thrown out with the garbage. In my mother's suitcases, I found only one snapshot of Roman Blueglass; I suspect it survived only because in it he was holding me. I was looking a little tearful with Uncle Roman's hands around my waist, as if he had just scared me by suddenly lifting me up with my bare legs dangling any which way. He had curly gray hair and a sardonic vulpine face I almost remember.

To my aunt, Roman Blueglass must have seemed a godsent rescuer, coming along when she was in her forties, long after she had resigned herself to never meeting anyone worthwhile. He removed her at once from Mapleton, from her mother and Leona, and bore her away to Bay Ridge—a more elegant Brooklyn neighborhood of Mediterranean-style villas that overlooked the waters of the Narrows and a brand-new promenade called Shore Road. Polo was played on Sundays at nearby Fort Hamilton. They found a big cheap apartment in a six-story red-brick building at 74 Gatling Place, for which they bought a lot of dark, serious-looking furniture. The *Encyclopaedia Britannica,* the complete works of Henrik Ibsen and George Bernard Shaw, including *A Young Woman's Guide to Socialism,* illustrated editions of Balzac's *Droll Tales* and *Candide,* as well as various books and pamphlets by Leon Trotsky, filled a pair of handsome mahogany bookcases in the living room.

In his spare time, Roman Blueglass fooled around with cameras. He must have felt quite gratified when he won a "best picture of the month" contest at the New York Institute of Photography. Setting up lights around the Bay Ridge apartment, he did ambitiously artistic studies of groupings of objects, often focusing upon two Art Deco figurines—naked maidens, impossibly slender, delicately balanced on one toe. In one of his studies, he positioned his wife between them. With the maidens poised on end tables on either

side of her as if about to take flight, Anna, a solid middle-aged figure in a dark dress, occupies a plush armchair as well as her husband's attention, her contentment palpable as she surveys, almost
with disbelief, the new home they have made together.

One Saturday afternoon, Rosalind and Anna met on Thirty-
fourth Street and went to Macy's together. That day there was a
huge cash-and-carry sale of what would later be known as Depression glass—complete sets in a variety of colors. The store was
practically giving the stuff away. The incredibly low prices made
the two recent brides giddy. Anna fell in love with a pink set; Rosalind was enraptured by a green one. There were glasses for wine,
water, cordial; pitchers suitable for iced tea; footed compotes for
fruit; enormous platters where you could lay out an array of crust-
less sandwiches. With the right glassware, you could entertain on

the grand scale. They didn't quite know whom they were going to invite over except each other, but they each bought a set in anticipation of all the festivities permanently called off by the Depression.

For the first time in her adult life, Rosalind was living in Manhattan. She was actually within walking distance of Mme Ziegler's, but it had been years since her voice training had ended, and it would have been painful to run into the old lady. The girls she'd met at the Academy of Normal Singing had all scattered, most of them vanishing into marriage, though once or twice she recognized a name in the music section of the paper. Sometimes she felt she didn't know anyone. Even Caroline Robinson had stopped writing.

The apartment Dan had found them on West Sixty-fifth Street was dark even on sunny days and so small that the new piano took up most of the living room, leaving barely enough space for a sofa and a dinette set. It was a long subway ride from there to Mapleton and an even longer one to Bay Ridge. She had always complained about her mother and sisters, longed for the time when she could have a life of her own, but more and more she found that she missed them, especially Anna, who often seemed completely swallowed up by her demanding husband with his many unpredictable moods.

Dan didn't have moods the way Roman did. He was always considerate and affectionate, with words of praise for every meal she cooked. He had wanted an old-fashioned double bed, but had given in to her request that they have twin ones instead, in the new fashion, with a sweet little maple night table that matched the headboards in between. He understood that she had always been a light sleeper, very easily disturbed; she'd made him see also that

double beds led to babies, and it would be a while before they
could afford one.

In some ways, although she hated to admit it, being married
and always knowing what to expect was boring. When you were
single, uncertainty about the future—all the suspense about meeting or not meeting someone—kept you on your toes. On her visits
to Shreveport and Dallas when she was terribly young and awfully
scared, she had felt her life as a story unfolding. She had never expected an ending that would take the form of a treadmill, where
you were always washing the same dishes, vacuuming the same
rug, hearing the same weekend drone of the ballgame on the
radio.

Still, all in all, she supposed she was happy. Who could be
happy every minute?

Sometimes her husband had to leave her and go out of town for
several days. The Metropolitan Tobacco Company had branches
in Patchogue and Asbury Park. They would send him out to take
inventory and check the books. It was part of the job, he explained
to her. To tell the truth, it was the part he particularly relished. He
liked having a chance to play detective, looking for discrepancies
in the accounts, hoping there wouldn't be any, of course, but
sometimes human nature got the better of people. He'd ride out
on the train with another chap from the office, sit in the smoking
car, and play gin rummy. By now he knew all the men in the
branches, and he'd go out with some of them in the evenings.
Sometimes they had introduced him to girls. But that was before
Rosalind.

Thinking about her from a distance, imagining her rattling
around in the silent apartment, sitting down at the dinette table all

alone opposite his empty chair, gave him sort of a lump in the throat. He knew it wasn't fair that he should enjoy himself without her. It didn't take much for him to have a good time—a decent cigar, a victory for the Brooklyn Dodgers, the small illicit thrill of placing a two-dollar bet on the races at Jamaica. A Sunday outing to Rockaway with Roz was the kind of thing that would pep him up for the entire week—he wanted the two of them to have outings every Sunday, provided the weather cooperated. You could be happy even without much money, if you had each other. At least, this was true for him. But he had begun to feel that Roz needed more, that being married to him wasn't quite enough for her, particularly whenever he had to leave her on her own.

A year after their wedding, to his great relief, a solution presented itself. In Anna's building in Bay Ridge, an apartment suddenly became vacant—it was not only larger and sunnier but less expensive than the one they had. My father didn't especially care to see more of his brother-in-law Roman, who struck him as a cold fish, but here was the ideal opportunity to reunite Roz with her sister.

All the benefits of their upcoming departure from Manhattan, including the greenery and superior fresh air of Brooklyn, looked better and better to my father during the week he had to spend in Patchogue that August. "The moving is constantly on my mind," he wrote my mother, "and now that we have definitely decided, it makes me very happy, in fact I am thrilled about it and impatient to get it over. I like it especially as when I am away you won't be so lonesome. I am sure it will turn out to be a new life for us."

The new apartment had a tiny second bedroom, which they would leave empty until such time as they needed to buy a crib.

Their still deferred, shadowy child was perhaps in my father's thoughts as he commented upon *Bedtime Story*, a Maurice Chevalier movie he and another fellow had seen in Patchogue the night before: "Stuffier than usual but entertaining. I think you would enjoy it, however, as there is a cute little baby on display, which would appeal to you."

The summer Anna and Rosalind finally married, Uda had to cable his congratulations. Fed up with the Depression and his encounters with anti-Semitism in the States, he had taken a job with Western Electric in Lima, Peru, bringing talking pictures and radio to Latin America; when they inquired about his religion on their application form, he wrote "Protestant" with no compunction.

Life in Peru brought out the romantic side of Uda's nature. In Mapleton, he had startled the neighborhood by bringing home an Amazonian green monkey as a house pet; for a time he had taken up flying as a weekend hobby despite the fears of his mother and sisters. In Lima, soon after his arrival, he met a stunning woman, unhappily married to a crooked politician. It took him three years to convince Julia Moral Hernandez to get a divorce; immediately afterward, giving her no time to change her mind, he eloped with her to Cartagena. Julia's two bewildered daughters accompanied them on their wedding trip—to pacify the little girls, he bought them diamond earrings.

The letters he sent home addressed to "Dear Folks" were long but essentially uncommunicative, full of advice as to how his sisters should improve their lives; he might casually refer to an alarming event such as an earthquake, but he never mentioned Julia.

My mother first learned of Uda's marriage in April 1934 in a letter he sent off just before boarding a Grace Line steamer with his new wife and stepdaughters for a visit to New York: "I am writing to you Rosalind to help me prepare the folks and to keep them from having hysterics. I am thirty-six," he pointed out, "and have done everything in my right mind. I have picked the woman who can keep me contented. She is thirty-four years of age, brunette, with a classic face, Greek profile, very well built, graceful, tiny feet. She has wonderful taste, and like you, she makes her own clothes. She has the makings of a good pianist but has neglected the piano due to an unhappy marriage.

"While not Jewish," Uda admitted anxiously, "she has Jewish blood. She is of Portuguese descent on both sides, so don't think for a minute that she is a Lupe Valdez or Indian. As a matter of fact, she looks and acts Jewish. Fat and ugly as I am, I am very lucky to have persuaded her to marry me."

A photo was enclosed of a voluptuous stranger, radiantly smiling at the cameraman, one hand flirtatiously on her hip, the other attempting to secure a windswept pompadour of black hair. She did not look Jewish to Uda's sisters; moreover, she wore makeup and was a divorcée. From their scrutiny of their new sister-in-law, they could only conclude that their infatuated brother had lost his head.

Six months later they forgave Uda a little when he wrote to them from Lima, announcing the birth of a son. Baby fever had struck the family. My mother decided that even if the Depression lasted forever, she could no longer put off trying to get pregnant. On September 27, 1935, she had my father triumphantly cable Uda that I had just been born. "At last you have something of your own!" he cabled back.

They called me Joyce in memory of Samuel Rosenberg. Uda seemed surprised that they would name their baby girl after his father and held forth about it in his next letter in a deliberately unsentimental way. "I didn't see the connection until I started to deduce things à la Sherlock Holmes and finally traced the Joyce to joy and then to its Hebrew equivalent and then to Samuel."

His jocular tone suggested that the whole question of paying homage to the dead made him extremely uncomfortable. He was proud to have named his son Alan after no one in particular.

When the newborn infant was brought home from the hospital and installed in the apartment downstairs from his on Gatling Place, Roman Blueglass found a new subject for his experiments with photography. Imitating Muybridge, he did a sequence of twenty-four shots of the sleeping baby under its blanket, the position of the small round head shifting ever so slightly from picture to picture. He mounted them on black cardboard for his puzzled in-laws. A candid shot of mother and child, with Rosalind looking haggard and suddenly much older after her ordeal in the hospital but very proud and pleased, was more traditional. I instantly recognize the mother in that photo, but the infant could be anyone's baby—I could not have picked myself out of a lineup.

When I look at a photo taken several months later, something stirs. Incredibly moon-faced by then, I am sitting up in a baby carriage looking around me at the world; just behind me is the brick wall of what I am almost sure is 74 Gatling Place—it seems to me that I remember that wall, how the red glowed from inside the bricks when the sunlight fell upon it.

My first strong memory of myself dates from the time when I must have just recently learned to walk. I was alone in a jungle of grass, each blade with its waving tassel of seeds high above my head—there was the entirely new and pleasurable feeling of being lost and wanting to remain lost, with the warm green stems buzzing and humming all around me. From a distance, a woman's voice kept futilely trying to summon me back as I went deeper into the jungle.

For some reason, I always placed that field of unmown grass in Maine—had I been brought there on my parents' vacation?—until I found a snapshot saved by my mother marked "Great Torrington, Connecticut." Part of my jungle is in the foreground; behind it is the porch of an old country house, where my mother in a long, flowered housecoat has me firmly by the arm. Perhaps it was taken minutes after my adventure, my attempted getaway.

Uda took delight in everything his baby did, even in things that were hardly accomplishments: "He likes to bite my ear and then laugh out loud. Yesterday I let him bite my ear just once and he bit me quite hard, so I guess we won't play that game again." By the time the boy was two, Uda couldn't help bragging to my mother, "The doctor says he is very very exceptional and intelligent. We think he is going to be some sort of genius. He is, of course, the joy of our existence."

The joy of my mother's existence came with unanticipated clouds and frustrations, although Uda had been right in recognizing how badly she needed something of her own. She was convinced that she had an even more superior baby than Uda's and couldn't wait to measure its IQ. When her daughter started talking very early, she was thrilled. But unfortunately the child talked incessantly, shutting up only when it fell asleep. She made it the most adorable outfits, but of course it was totally indifferent to what it wore, with a talent for making stains that would not come out in the wash. On bad days, the baby seemed like the good furniture she had to keep dusted, part of the treadmill. No one had warned her about the essential thanklessness of motherhood. Perhaps if she had not been the youngest in the family, if her own mother had not become a closed book, if Anna had not taken over her upbringing after Pa died and doted upon her so, she would have had a better idea of what to expect.

Yet she knew her sisters envied her. Of course, Leona, who could hardly boil water without burning the pot, would have been preposterous as a mother. But Anna had been born for it. She grieved for Anna, married too late for babies, tried as much as she could to share her daughter with her, as if the child were their new little sister and Rosalind herself had moved up in rank, somehow becoming the oldest one with her knowledge of labor and sore nipples and smelly diapers—a full-fledged woman now, while Anna and Leona remained "the girls."

*    *    *

I don't remember Roman Blueglass at all or the unusual agitation in the family when he pulled off his disappearing act, vanishing completely and inexplicably from my aunt's apartment on Gatling Place. I am guessing it happened in 1937, judging from a letter Uda wrote in the spring of '38, asking whether Anna's "pessimistic outlook" had lifted yet. Uda had been told that his sister lacked "an interest in life," and it was like him to come up with a practical, commonsense solution. Wouldn't taking up social work help Anna, even if it was unpaid? After all, Uda reasoned, "she does not have to worry, as she is all right in that she has a home and folks who look after her and care about her."

But Anna was not all right, and it couldn't have helped to hear from her brother how many other people in the United States "were in the same boat," awaiting the better times that were "just around the corner."

By the time I was three, I knew enough to give my aunt extra kisses and let her hold me as long as she wanted to whenever she came downstairs to visit us. "Anna has a broken heart," I heard my mother remark to my father. I pictured it looking like the cracked vase my mother could no longer use for flowers after I accidentally knocked it to the floor.

She was a woman who had lost everything in a day. After giving birth at forty-five to a stillborn infant, Anna had nearly died after an embolism. When she came to after a series of operations, Roman Blueglass was nowhere to be found, and her savings had vanished with him. She hired a detective to look for Roman, but the trail petered out somewhere in Canada. My aunt changed her name back to Anna Ross and got a job keeping books for Gingham Girl, a manufacturer of housecoats and aprons. I grew up assuming Aunt Anna was an old maid like Aunt Leona.

I heard Roman's name for the first time when I was fourteen. In Hunter High School I had made the acquaintance of a dashing group of older girls who told me they were Trotskyites, or at least their boyfriends were; once they took me along with them to the Village to sell *The Militant* after school. Visiting my aunt soon after this adventure, my eye fell upon an old red book, *My Life* by Leon Trotsky. I had never taken any particular notice of it before. In fact, I had no idea anyone in my uncolorful, ordinary family had ever been interested in Trotsky.

"Oh, yes," Aunt Anna said, "my husband was quite involved with him in Russia."

"Your *husband?*" I asked, astounded. "What happened to him?"

"Ran off," she said after a moment's hesitation. "I used to tell myself he feared for his life—they assassinated Trotsky, you know. But I think Roman was just a rotten human being—there are men who do terrible things and women who are foolish enough to marry them."

"That book—," Aunt Anna said, "I don't know why I keep it, and there are pamphlets taking up room in the closet. What do I need them for? I should throw them out."

"Can I look at them someday?"

"Be my guest," my aunt said, so bitterly I never got around to it.

So that Anna wouldn't have to be alone, my grandmother and Leona sold the house in Mapleton and moved into Anna's apartment. My grandmother slept in the twin bed Roman had vacated and spent her days cooking enormous meals her eldest daughter had no appetite for. Leona took over the second bedroom, from which my father had removed the crib, arriving with her golf clubs, her tennis trophies, and an exercycle. She filled the air with

cigarette smoke and gave Anna headaches by banging out tunes on
the sour keys of the old Sohmer upright my mother had left behind when she married.

The family was reconstituted, the sisters reunited, with my father taking Uda's place as the household male. The sisters took the
stairs to each other's apartments, which seemed more private than
taking the elevator. In the evenings, there was constant traffic up
and down. Anna was distracted from her tragedy not by social
work but by the revival of her irritation with Leona. Leona ran to
my mother to complain about Anna's latest insult. My grandmother got in the habit of coming downstairs, too, installing herself on our living-room sofa with my father's newspaper folded
under her black shoes and falling instantly asleep. My father
started taking very long after-dinner walks, citing his need to
smoke his cigar in fresh air. There were too many women in his
life—he wanted to be married to only one of them.

My grandmother fed me calf's-foot jelly and butter cookies over
my mother's objections and promised she'd dance at my wedding.
She talked to her steaming pots in a secret language. My mother
said it was praying. "Cursing is more like it," said Leona with a
laugh. "What's cursing?" I asked. My mother gave Leona a vexed
look and answered, "Whatever." "Putting the Evil Eye on Grand-
ma's enemies," Leona volunteered. "What's an Evil Eye?" "Nothing," my mother said coldly. "Nothing at all."

I liked going up to Aunt Anna's apartment. I liked belonging to
many grown-ups and getting more presents that way. But the thing
I wanted most—one of the iconic Deco objects left behind by
Roman Blueglass—Aunt Anna couldn't give me. It was a translucent blue girl who sat at the edge of a blue pool wearing no cloth-
ing. Sometimes I found it necessary to defend her from violation

by pleading with my father not to stub out his cigar in the ripples of water in which she was about to immerse her toes.

In my aunt's foggy living room, where all the doleful browns and greens merged with the gray rising up from the carpet, two other sprightly girls, whom I sometimes tried to imitate, balanced on the points of their toes. But the blue girl was far more beautiful. I was enchanted by the way she stretched out her slender legs, rhapsodically tilting back her head, smiling at some source of pleasure deep inside herself as her pointy glass breasts caught the light. "Why is she smiling?" I asked my mother.

"Because she's very, very happy."

"Why is she so very happy?"

My mother sighed, as she often did when she feared I was launching into a series of overlapping questions. This time, I'd apparently stumped her—for some reason, she seemed particularly hard put to come up with an answer.

"Because, Miss Chatterbox," she said, her cheeks flushing, "her mother's about to give her a nice warm bath."

As my vocabulary grew by leaps and bounds, Aunt Leona became my devoted scribe. She would follow me around, collecting my sayings in shorthand, later typing them up at the office. Carbons would be given out to her friends and even mailed to Uncle Uda so that my sayings could be circulated in Peru. Aunt Leona was ecstatic when at four I dictated my first poem—"Birds can fly/Why can't I?"—overlooking the degree to which it had been influenced by the new popular song "Over the Rainbow."

Pleased that a few simple words could generate so many hugs and kisses, I came up on the spot with a longer and more ambitious poem that was somewhat less derivative:

> *Sleep, baby, sleep*
> *My mother watches the dreams*
> *The flowers grow right on the lawn*
> *The snow is fallen nice and clean*
>     *on the lawn*
> *Oh green! Oh green!*
> *Sleep, baby, sleep.*

Aunt Leona rushed this one to my mother. Cuteness was one thing, but for four years they had been on the alert for the moment when Samuel Rosenberg's lost brilliance would speak to them through me. They immediately made an appointment at Teachers College to have my IQ tested there.

*The Book of Joyce Alice Glassman by Her Aunt Leona Ross,* for which Leona fortunately failed to find a publisher, contains some stuff I find revealing. Quite early I seem to have been perplexed by a strange imbalance in my family. Men and women seemed to come in twos, so where were the men for my deserving aunts? Whenever the fleet came into the Brooklyn Navy Yard, handsome sailors, who seemed to lack wives, appeared in our neighborhood in their striking uniforms. I suggested to Leona that they'd make perfect husbands for herself and Anna.

I was also more than willing to share my mother with another child—a recurring motif in *The Book of Joyce Alice Glassman.* Each time Mother went to the doctor, I hoped we would learn that a tiny seed had been planted under her heart. It must have seemed the only way I would be allowed have a playmate in the house. By the time I was six, though, I was either somewhat brainwashed or all too accustomed to playing to my audience: "Another child would interfere with my career," I told Aunt Leona.

A more authentic voice is heard in the following bit of recorded dialogue with Mother, where what Mother says gets to the crux of an emerging struggle that would eventually drive us apart:

JOYCE: *Mother, all the boys and girls laugh at me. I can't cross the street or go into anybody's house.*

MOTHER: *Well, Joyce, what if you did cross the street? There is nothing more there.*

It was the age of pernicious, supposedly scientific child-rearing practices when infants were left to howl until their scheduled feeding times and conscientious mothers like mine exhausted themselves conducting warfare on the germs that lurked in every mote of dust. My mother's bible was a book called *Healthy Babies Are Happy Babies.* Healthy babies apparently moved their bowels right after breakfast and ate every scrap on their plates. I remember my mother's distress when I failed to perform as expected and my terror of the hideous orange rubber enema bag that hung like impending doom on the bathroom door. I remember a period when for some reason I had no appetite and was made to sit for hours at the kitchen table mournfully chewing larger and larger mouthfuls I was unable to swallow. Gradually I began to sense that there were different kinds of love—that my father and Aunt Anna loved me just because I was there, that Aunt Leona needed something from me that I seemed to have plenty of—words she could carry away in her pocketbook. But my mother's exacting love depended upon my bodily functions being as perfect as the rest of my behavior.

Most of the time, our days together went smoothly enough. When I wasn't looking at picture books in my room, she would dress me in one of the outfits I was afraid to soil because it was so much nicer than what ordinary little girls wore, and we would head for Shore Road to get as much fresh air as we could.

I last walked on Shore Road a half century ago, but at various times, driving past it, I've stared in surprise at the lush foliage of the old trees, which make the park such a green, well-shaded place that it bears no resemblance to the one I knew in my childhood—

a strip of gray hexagonal paving stones and solitary benches, its newly planted saplings, hardly older than I was, restrained by poles and wires with tan leggings wrapped around their spindly trunks. What I can't recall is seeing any children at play on Shore Road, though of course there must have been a few. In fact, the barren

park I remember only bears out my mother's point that if you crossed the street, you'd find nothing.

I was usually allowed to dig sedately in the hard dirt around the new trees, but I was not allowed to run or climb. My mother had convinced herself that my skin was exceptionally delicate and had to be protected from permanent scarring. Sometimes small white or yellow flowers, not part of the official plan for Shore Road, would appear in the cracks between the paving stones; these, my mother told me, were wild and belonged to no one. Picking dandelions and clover and making them into bouquets for her became my passion; it was my greatest hope that sooner or later we would come upon a flower I had never seen.

The high point of my day was my father's return from the Metropolitan Tobacco Company. Soon after we got back from the park, I would begin waiting, running back and forth to the door to listen for the elevator that would stop, slide open, and deliver him to me. The moment I heard his key in the lock, I would be ready to overwhelm him, grabbing his hat as he bent down to me, rubbing my cheek against his raspy face, still cold from outside. With my arms tight around him, he would scoop me up and head for the kitchen, eager for my mother's polite, anticlimactic kiss.

Evidently somebody must have noticed that I was spending too much of my time with adults, because soon after my visit to Teachers College I found myself in the backyard of a private house in the midst of children—children who were running, climbing, riding around on tricycles, biting, hitting, getting grape jelly and finger paint all over their clothes. I have a very clear memory of myself standing in the middle of a porch glider, loaded with kids on either side, that is rocking wildly back and forth. Everybody is shrieking with delight, and I am the most enthusiastic of the shriekers—in fact, I have gotten all the others to shriek with me, and I jump up and down on the swaying floor because I have never felt quite so wonderful. I could go on like this forever, but a furious woman comes running and stops the glider. Dragging me off it, she yells, "If you ever do that again, I'll spank you with a hammer!" And I never did it again. In fact, I have tended to stand back and look on ever since.

That was nursery school—not exactly Montessori. Usually the proprietress, a woman whose husband had lost everything in the stock market, sat with her head in her hands, letting nature take its course. I was indignantly removed from there by Mother in the middle of a Christmas pageant, when she was horrified to see me in a green crepe paper costume singing "Silent Night" as I held a lighted candle. I can still remember the interesting feeling of the hot wax dripping on my wrist.

I was never told why my parents decided to leave Gatling Place, what they hoped to achieve by moving a few blocks away. Perhaps it was meant to be a cure for the sinus headaches my mother had started complaining about, or their second attempt to establish a new life—this time by putting a bit of distance between my mother and her family. The new address, One-two-three Marine Avenue, which I had to memorize in case I ever got lost, still rings in my mind like a counting rhyme.

Our new four-room apartment was in a six-story brick building that stood out like a sore thumb in a neighborhood of graceful wooden houses with tidy lawns bordered by flowering bushes. On the corner, surrounded by chestnut trees, was a rambling old brown-shingled place that I thought of as a "mansion" because of its round tower. Looking down from my new room, I'd often see a boy in the yard, crouching in the grass, then suddenly springing forward, ready to shoot his invisble enemies with a rifle.

Now that I would soon be a first-grader, my mother would put me on the elevator and let me go outside by myself as long as I stayed directly in front of our building. I'd wheel my doll carriage back and forth, paying little attention to the celluloid baby inside, hoping some real child would come along. Soon we had learned that I was not only one of the few small children on the block, but unfortunately the only girl.

All my mother's social life seemed to take place between floors in the elevator. Ladies would smile at us and try to strike up conversations. By then the possibility of war was beginning to replace the weather as a topic of common interest. I would hear the names Hitler, Warsaw, Czechoslovakia, and one day a woman said, "I hope we do get into a war. I think it will serve us right," so vehemently that I worried for a while about why we had to be punished, since I knew something about the consequences of being "served right." The opinionated woman's name was Paula. She wore purple slacks and had hair my mother said was "dark at the roots." She wanted my mother to attend a lecture with her.

"Why don't you go?" my father said that night.

"Because I'd rather not get involved. She's just the kind of person who'll be ringing the bell all the time for this and that."

Which was exactly what Paula did for a while. My mother was willing to stand in the doorway and chat, but would never invite her inside. Apart from my aunts and my grandmother and my father's relatives, whom we didn't see very often, only the super and the Fuller Brush man were welcome visitors.

My mother was waiting for her new living room to be perfect, so that she and my father could begin to entertain. Somehow the right sort of friends would materialize—after the drapes were bought on the installment plan, after the couch was reupholstered and the needlepoint cover for the piano bench was finished and the lampshades were replaced one by one.

Meanwhile I made the acquaintance of the boy from the brown-shingled mansion who played soldier. He came by one day and asked if I wanted to be in his army. I abandoned the doll carriage and followed him to his yard. He handed me a stick, and we crawled across his lawn together. Whenever he said so, I had to lie flat without moving because otherwise the enemy would get me. The lawn was rather wet and in some places had no grass.

That day I was wearing the new yellow dress Mother had just made me—as usual, I could have been presented at a ladies' tea party. I didn't notice the brown dirt down the front of my dress until I went upstairs. My mother took one look and slapped my face. She had never done anything like that before—no one ever had—and for a moment I was astonished. When she slapped me again, I hit back, striking her in the stomach, which was as far as I could reach. I hit her without even deciding to, as if my arm couldn't help it.

She pulled me into the bathroom, yanked off my dress and underpants, and made me get into the tub. To serve me right, she was going to tell my father, and he would punish me later. "Please don't tell Daddy! Please don't tell Daddy!" I kept screaming as she grimly scrubbed the dirt away, but she didn't seem to hear me.

For the first time I wished my father would never come home. I didn't understand what he had to do with what had happened between my mother and me or why I would also have to lose his love and he would have to lose mine. By the time he arrived, I had cried so much I was unable to eat the food in front of me. Sobbing and hiccupping, I sat at the table, waiting for my punishment to begin.

Whatever my father may have thought of my mother's approach to discipline, he did not object to his allotted task, although all through dinner he looked miserable. He ate a little vanilla pudding, had a sip or two of his coffee, then led me into the bathroom, sat down on the toilet, and put me over his knee. His hand descended on my bottom once, and I threw up all over him. I think he was relieved I had granted him the most convincing of all possible reasons to stop.

In my mother's papers, I was surprised to come upon an ancient pamphlet on how to punish children that she must have sent away for around that time. Spanking was considered less effective than verbally instilling a sense of shame. It's odd that my mother kept it for the next fifty years. It couldn't have been much use to her by the time I was eighteen and gave her flimsy excuses for staying out all night, or when I entered my Beat period and went off to the slums of the East Village to consort with Jack Kerouac and God knows who else and was hardly ever home when she called and, even when she reached me, uncommunicative. She may have wondered how she had produced a daughter who had become so unknowable and where the rift between us could have started—the invisible crack that must have been widening imperceptibly. Perhaps she sometimes took out *The Book of Joyce Alice Glassman* to reread the poem I wrote at eight at the height of my career as a child:

> *I would like to travel round the world*
> *on a plane*
> *But very soon come back again*
> *For one of Mother's kisses*

I doubt that she remembered the yellow dress.

As Mother obliviously vacuumed or ran the sewing machine upstairs, I slipped into a secret life on Marine Avenue. At its center was Alexander, the boy who lived on the corner. Although he was seven, too old and worldly-wise to be bothered with a five-year-old, he started coming for me whenever he needed a devoted follower.

Alexander had a devil-may-care attitude I very much admired and a dazzling ability to climb a tree in a flash. He'd scale a magnolia and exhort me to do likewise, pelting me with leaves and twigs as I stood awestruck on the ground, ashamed to explain that

I couldn't risk returning to Mother with telltale scars, that my underpants might show if I climbed. Apart from some occasional teasing, Alexander was inclined to be tolerant of my complete lack of athletic ability, but there were days when he wanted nothing to do with me because I was a girl.

Down the street lived Alex's friend Marshall, who claimed to know me from nursery school, although I had no recollection of him. He told Alex how disgracefully I had wept the day the teacher scolded me for showing off on the porch glider. Alex thought he could toughen me up. Marshall wanted Alex to himself. Often the two of them would resolve this running conflict by ganging up on me and ordering me to go home to my mother where I belonged.

Alex had an irresistibly tender side that would show itself when Marshall wasn't around. I remember some blissful hours in the kitchen of the brown-shingled house, making gingerbread men to go into a coal oven under the kindly supervision of Alex's grandmother, who, according to Alex, let him do anything he wanted. His father was forever away on business, and he didn't seem to have a mother. The house was very bare, compared to my mother's living room, and there was a damaged wing where we couldn't go because rain had come through the roof. In the backyard was a shed where you could look up through a hole in the ceiling and see a cloud float by or a patch of blue. I wanted to live there when Alex and I got married. We got into the habit of going into the shed to see what we looked like without our pants, as if we needed frequent verification in case anything had changed. Alex had an extra little teapot through which he could shoot pee in an arc. "Bet you can't do that," he said. And I couldn't.

Alex thought it was silly of me to keep picking the dandelions and clover that grew on his lawn. "Those aren't flowers," he'd say. "Those are just weeds." But I still considered them very beautiful.

One day he told me he knew where we could get lots of real flowers.

"Where?" I asked him.

"From other people's gardens."

He led me to a house around the corner and stood watch by the privet hedge as I plucked as many petunias and pansies as my hands could hold. He was helping me tug at a bush covered with pink blossoms when a furious fox terrier appeared and we had to run like hell, with a trail of petals dropping from my bouquet. Alex advised me to leave it in the shed so that I wouldn't get arrested, but I couldn't resist bringing it home to Mother.

"Where do these flowers come from?" she asked, sounding a little suspicious.

"A lady gave them to me," I answered after some quick thinking. The story, once I had said it, seemed to have its own truth.

"What a nice lady!"

Of course she forbade me to ever accept another present from a stranger. Still, she put my flowers in a vase instead of a mayonnaise jar and set them on the dinette table. When they wilted, my lie went with them into the garbage pail.

My relationship with Alex foundered when shortly before he went to visit his uncle in Maine, I failed a toughness test that he and Marshall had devised. They wanted me to walk up to the front door of a certain house across the street, ring the bell, and just stand there until the lady inside came out. But at the last minute, I lost my courage and fled.

Alex told me we were through forever. Not only that—he and his uncle were going to trap a bear and bring it back to Brooklyn. The bear would get me at the end of the summer. "Bears eat cowards," Marshall said. "They can smell a coward from three miles away."

I didn't ask my parents about the bear. It belonged to my secret life, which had somehow become more powerful and real than the one I had with them. I spent the summer convinced that my existence was trickling away. Mother worried that I seemed strangely quiet and kept taking my temperature.

By August I had almost grown used to the inevitability of my encounter with the bear. One morning I looked out the window and saw Alex playing in his yard. I also noticed that the door to the shed was ominously shut. I finished what I believed was my last bowl of breakfast cereal and went downstairs to get the whole thing over with.

To my amazement, Alexander seemed pleased to see me. He showed me how he could sharpen sticks with a penknife his uncle had given him and even offered me a try.

"But what about the bear?" I finally asked him.

"What bear?"

How could Alexander have forgotten something that to me was a matter of life and death? I didn't know what to make of that. But I knew I was very lucky he still liked me.

Fifteen years later, the phone rang in the brownstone apartment near Columbia University where I'd been living for several months. Just a year ago, I'd left home. A man with a slight southern accent asked hesitantly if he was speaking to Joyce Glassman. "Are you the Joyce who used to live on Marine Avenue?"

"Yes," I said in astonishment, "but I was only around six at the time."

"Well, this is Alexander."

He'd just moved back up north, he explained, and was about to start engineering school at Columbia. The other day he'd gone out to Brooklyn for a look at the old neighborhood and had found himself wondering what had happened to the kids he'd known on Marine Avenue. He hadn't been able to trace Marshall, but when he looked through the Glassmans in the Manhattan phone book, he couldn't believe it—there I was, just a few blocks away. "I don't know anyone in New York," he admitted plaintively. "Not a soul."

"Look, why don't you just come over?" I said. It was one of those nights when I was grateful for company.

When I opened the door a half hour later, a gangly young man in a seersucker suit with a painfully innocent face and a painfully short blond crew cut was standing in the hall. I could no longer remember how Alexander used to look, but I was unable to superimpose this stranger upon his teasing, darting shadow.

He seemed somewhat taken aback to find me in an apartment of my own. "You live here by yourself?" he asked incredulously.

I watched Alexander slowly take in the room—the dark knobby furniture that had come with the place, the three-burner stove in the corner, the prints from Picasso's Blue Period tacked to the wall, the quite unmissable double bed. I could have sworn his ears turned red as he regarded my sleeping arrangements. The year was 1956—just before so much began to change. Somehow I had rushed ahead of him and had one foot in the future.

When he asked me about my life, I didn't say too much, only that I was working as a secretary in a literary agency (I had to explain what that was) and hoped to become a writer myself, as evidenced by a Royal portable out on a table and the untidy stacks of books on the carpetless floor. Compared to the old shed with its views of sky, the place was pretty unromantic. It had an unfixable melancholy that seemed to go with the blue period that had started after a love affair that had gone wrong and a bleak trip to Canarsie for an abortion earlier that summer. I hadn't thought as much about mortality since I'd been five years old.

Unlike Alexander, I felt no nostalgia for my childhood. At any time I could have taken a subway to Bay Ridge, but I'd never even considered it. I preferred to view my own years there as a source of weird material. Alexander's nonexistent bear had stayed in my head, and my funny obsession with dandelions and clover. And there was another Bay Ridge episode that had potential, if I ever figured out what it really meant. It was as close as I'd ever come to a mystical experience, not that I believed in that kind of thing.

It must have taken place in the fall, very soon after I'd started first grade. I could remember my pretty young teacher saying she hoped someone in the class would bring her a cosmos from their garden because it would be a very easy flower for children to draw. I felt ashamed to have no garden and not even to know what a cosmos was.

Now that I was six, I was allowed to walk back and forth to school along Marine Avenue by myself. Each day I'd pass a lot where a house had once burned to the ground. There was nothing left but some blackened bricks that lay amongst tall dry weeds and a couple of steps leading nowhere. The following morning I went by there as usual. On a long stem a mauve flower had blossomed overnight, above a cluster of hard red buds and feathery leaves. Something impelled me to take it with me to school. The teacher identified it. Miraculously, I had found a cosmos. The memory had remained with me as a sort of touchstone, as if the cosmos had been a sign of some ultimate benevolence in the scheme of things.

My childhood had certainly been lonely and peculiar, but Alexander's had turned out to be even more of a mess than mine. I could see how life had changed him into this fellow who seemed so unsure of himself and knew so little. When he was ten, he came home from school and found his grandmother dead. His father sold the house quickly and took him down south, where he was looking for work. For a couple of years they lived in a series of boardinghouses. Finally, the father married again and settled down to start another family, but Alexander had been sent away to military school. No wonder he told me he'd always missed Brooklyn. It was too bad, I thought, that Brooklyn was all we had in common.

I asked him whether One-two-three Marine Avenue was still there. He said it looked pretty much the same, but the house where he'd lived with his grandmother had been torn down and replaced by more apartments. Even the chestnut trees on the corner were gone—he figured some kind of blight must have wiped them out. He was still determined to find Marshall.

Shortly before Alexander left that night, he asked my permission to talk about a problem that was weighing on his mind. "I'd like to know what you think," he said urgently, "but I don't want to offend you." For some reason he had decided to trust me.

"Don't worry. I'm not very shockable," I said, doubting that he could have a really dark secret.

About an hour ago, I had offered him a mug of instant coffee that he seemed to be unable to put down. Gripping it with both hands, he told me the bare bones of what had happened to him in Florida that spring on a fishing trip with his father—how he had met an extremely friendly older man in a Hawaiian shirt one evening on the beach when everyone was down there playing their radios and taking pictures of the sunset. The man had invited Alexander to join him at a bar and had later made a pass at him, kissed him on the lips to be exact. He had been asking himself ever since whether this meant he was a homosexual. Could the man have possibly seen something in him?

"Seen what?" I asked. "What could he have seen?"

"Something—something I didn't know was there."

I assured Alexander he was in agony over nothing, that it was just an accidental encounter, that the man had obviously made a mistake. "Just try and forget the whole thing," I advised him firmly, from the heights of my wisdom.

He put down the mug, thanked me politely for listening to him, and promised to call me very soon. A few weeks later, I saw him on Broadway, but he looked away so that he wouldn't have to greet me.

I was sick of men—sick in particular of those who preferred not to know you after they'd revealed too much about themselves. But maybe, I thought suddenly, Alexander really was gay, and had been trying to find a way to tell someone. If so, it was awful that I'd failed him. For a while I looked for him when I walked around the neighborhood, but I never ran into him again.

Among the poems about fairies and maidens, "Twinkling Sabbath candles small" and "Ruth, Ruth, loving and loyal," I find an early attempt at satirical realism in *The Book of Joyce Alice Glassman*. It's a monologue I composed when I was eleven, based upon my recollections of Mme Maria Ley Piscator, a prima donna from the Vienna stage, who had run the children's workshop in dramatic movement in which Mother enrolled me when I was eight. I had never seen a grown-up behave in such a flamboyant manner, stalking about on high heels, flinging up her arms, screaming "Vat is the dee-*fi*-culty?" with a beringed hand striking her forehead when one of us made a little mistake. She would often compare us most unfavorably with someone called Sarah Bernhardt as we stood shivering before her, barefoot in our abbreviated rayon tunics.

My monologue probably does Mme Piscator some injustice, but I can't help feeling it was essentially on the mark: "Ven you are sad, you must beat your chest zo. You must create graceful gestures with your hands—zis creates a beautiful background for vot you are doing. If you vant to be a natural character actress, you must have *millions* of gestures, you must *stress* gestures. Zay are ze basis of acting—more important zan ze vords. . . ."

Mme Piscator's pedagogy tended to be punctuated by impatient stampings of the foot and frequent utterances of the word *stupeed*, but in a way I think I admired her. I remember waiting in appalled fascination to see what she would do next.

I fell into Mme Piscator's hands after Mother took me to the New School for Social Research to see an expressionistic production of a children's play called *The Kings of Nomania* in which actors kept popping up on little platforms and tearing through the audience in full costume. I found it all tremendously exciting, and when Mother said, "Wouldn't you like to do that yourself someday?" I could think of nothing I'd like to do better, at least at the moment.

That very afternoon, Mme Piscator—all Viennese charm on this occasion—signed me up for her tutelage. Squeezing my round chin, she predicted a "future," though not necessarily stardom. My mother would subsequently claim that I had *begged* her to let me be in the theater, and that out of maternal love she had acquiesced, despite the self-sacrifice that it would involve.

She had exposed me to the theater once before when I was too young to appreciate it. It was a production of *Rip Van Winkle* at the Brooklyn Academy of Music. I still remember my horror when Rip awoke from his twenty-year nap with a long white beard. "This is not for little girls!" I'd loudly protested, and had to be shushed and removed from the premises. But I'd liked the way the lights dimmed and made everything quiet just before the velvet curtain began to glow.

I remember Mother telling Mme Piscator that I already had "experience"—by which she meant a couple of neighborhood dance recitals. I had been taught a bit of tap dancing, which had recently been popularized by Shirley Temple, and something resembling ballet, which unfortunately I was required to practice for an hour each day. I found it very boring compared to the whirling scarf dances I improvised to entertain my father when he played the Victrola after dinner.

I soon noticed that Mother always seemed especially cheerful on Saturdays when we went to the New School, though she complained about the long subway ride and having to hang around and wait for me, passing time in the cafeteria with the other mothers. She would get dressed up and put on lipstick (the only makeup she ever wore) and roll her hair into a pompadour (I had a smaller one on the left side of my forehead to set off my long braids). Sometimes we'd have egg salad sandwiches at a lunch counter on Fourteenth Street, where an aproned man would always say, "You two must be sisters." My mother would get pink in the face whenever Mme Piscator's husband, the silver-haired director of *The Kings of Nomania*, said hello to us. She told me Erwin Piscator was a great man, that before he came to America, he had worked with Max Reinhardt, and she took me to the movies one Saturday to see the Max Reinhardt production of *A Midsummer Night's Dream* and bought a recording of Mendelssohn's music for me to dance to. Though I didn't realize it, she must have felt that she was finally returning to the element in which she belonged. I had become the vehicle for that.

Because of my previous training, I was somewhat more adept at executing Mme Piscator's histrionic gestures than other little girls in the class. The dropout rate was impressive. Before long half the students had disappeared. "Now ve vill *really* concentrate," Mme Piscator said proudly. "Ve vill vork, vork, vork." Perhaps to ensure my continued enrollment, she told Mother I was her "little Pavlova" and gave me a chocolate truffle.

Down in the New School cafteria, rumors of an incredible new venture for the Piscators circulated through the dwindling group of coffee-drinking mothers—the establishment of a permanent children's theater on Broadway. For the smaller roles, most of the actors would be drawn from Erwin Piscator's workshop for adults, but there might be some opportunities for little girls. It seemed too thrilling to be true when Mme Piscator told my mother they could use me as a dancer in their first production, *Bobino,* which she herself would direct. Unfortunately, I wasn't to be given any lines, but what could be more eloquent than dramatic movement? It would hardly take up any of my time, Mme Piscator promised.

We had left Marine Avenue a few months before and moved to Kew Gardens in Queens. It seemed we had been living too close to the water for my mother's health. I suspect it was the start of my theatrical career that finally made her sinus headaches disappear altogether.

I felt lonely in Kew Gardens. I'd been taken away from Alexander and hadn't met any kid I liked as much. My one playmate was a girl in our new building who claimed that all Jews had big noses, but who slipped me a few of her Bobbsey Twin books nonetheless. I seemed to have nothing but time—the endless, not very precious time of a child—the placid routines of third grade, the weekly ballet lessons and visits to the public library, the reading I did in my room until Mother insisted I turn out the light. As far as the kids in third grade were concerned, too much about me was different— the clothes that made me look too dressed up, my rarefied diet of illustrated classics, my inability to ride a bike, my dearth of experience with ordinary stuff—bubble gum, soda pop, roller skates, Nancy Drew. I was becoming more and more aware of a kid culture all around me that I had no way of breaking into, no matter how many fairy poems I wrote. When Mme Piscator took all my time for *Bobino,* I didn't feel I'd lost a thing.

\* \* \*

The play the Piscators had chosen was about a wunderkind in some mythical European kingdom who preferred conversing with animals to learning Latin and Greek. There was to be a sizable chorus of wild and barnyard animals for which musical numbers had been written by a former disciple of Alban Berg's. Several of the other artists the Piscators had involved in their American Theater for Young Folks were also people who had once had reputations in Paris or Dresden or Basel or Berlin. Perhaps it was the bitter weight of all that formerness, combined with Mme Piscator's mad perfectionism and lack of tact, that put everyone on edge and made the stakes seem so high. Rehearsals would go on into the night, with operatic clashes between Mme Piscator and insulted and exhausted members of the cast, who would even threaten to walk out. "Then I am leaving, too!" Madame would rage back, exiting in high dudgeon. The following day Mr. Piscator would appear in his black cape to calm things down.

I remember drinking innumerable containers of hot chocolate brought to me by Mother as I waited from morning till night for Mme Piscator to need me, although I was only in a couple of scenes. Often by the time we got back to Kew Gardens, my deserted father would be in his pajamas. I had been cast as Cupid and had to do a dance with a five-pound gilt bow as Bobino and Princess Celestina sat on a bench in the palace garden making the rippling hand gestures of mutual attraction at each other. I had mixed feelings about my role, since I knew Cupid was supposed to be a boy, but Mother said that didn't matter at my age. I wore yellow tights and a yellow leotard with padded wings attached to the shoulders. My braids were stuffed into a matching headdress of ruffled tulle; only my pompadour was allowed to show. The final touch—the paper ivy and dogwood from Woolworth's wreathed artistically around me—was an inspiration of Mother's.

I was also supposed to play a bear, but in typical fashion Mme Piscator changed her mind. "Ve need a *large* bear," she declared two weeks from the opening and gave my role to a handsome student actor named Marlon Brando, who had been cast as a giraffe, and made me a rabbit instead. I could see immediately that Marlon Brando was a far more convincing bear than I could have been; in fact, everyone was so pleased with his performance that a second role of a drunken soldier was quickly created for him. Amongst the animals, more reshufflings occurred, requiring the creation of last-minute costumes. Elaine Stritch, another student from Mr. Piscator's workshop who would later become famous, began as a tiger and ended up as a cow.

Half blind inside my papier-mâché rabbit mask, I'd stagger across the stage with the other animals in the big production number that had to be rehearsed over and over again, Cries of "No! *No!* NO!" from Mme Piscator would often bring everything to a standstill. The browbeaten pianist, who had formerly concertized throughout Italy, would have to take it from the top, so that Madame could once more belt out her inimitable rendition of "Ze animales are zick, each dog und cat und chick," demonstrating the movements of hip and foot and derriere we were too clumsy to reproduce.

During the final week of dress rehearsals, an inspector from the society for the Prevention of Cruelty to Children made a surprise visit to the Adelphi Theater. The stage manager came rushing backstage to hide me, yanking me away from Mother and shoving me into a broom closet. A very long time passed as I sat weeping in the dark on an upended bucket, wondering what the cruelty could have been, since my life would be ruined if I couldn't be in *Bobino*.

We were later told that not only had the Piscators failed to get a license for me, but that children of my age were not allowed to dance on Broadway. Mme Piscator, however, had simply assured the inspector that there was no child in the cast. "Valk through it! Valk through it!" she shouted hoarsely, striking her forehead during the next rehearsal. But for the opening she threw caution to the winds, and I did my dance in its full splendor. "The cutest cupid you ever saw," said a reviewer for the *Journal-American*. Mother bought a dozen copies and underlined that phrase in every one.

When *Bobino* closed after its two scheduled weeks of performances, I had a Social Security number, a Junior Equity card, and a new name, Joyce Alice Ross, which had been printed in the stagebill but unfortunately not mentioned in the review. *Joyce Alice Ross* felt funny to me—it was like the rabbit mask in which I couldn't recognize myself. But *Ross* was Mother's old name, and it meant a lot to her to let me have it for my own career. She told me I could still use *Glassman* for school—it just wouldn't do for the stage. "Believe me," she said, "I *know* the theater."

I returned to third grade just as the Easter bunny cutouts were being peeled off the windows and red tulips were going up. Valentine's Day and Washington's Birthday had come and gone. In fact, it was nearly three months since I'd been seen in school, but no one seemed very interested in where I'd been or in my adventures on Broadway. A girl who had liked me before *Bobino* whispered to some other girls that I was stuck-up, and the teacher seemed quite upset that I had missed the beginning of multiplication. She sent me home with extra homework and a note from the principal of P.S. 99 addressed to my mother.

Mother wouldn't tell me what was in the envelope I'd brought her, only that it was nothing I had to worry about. But before I fell asleep that night, I overheard her on the phone with Aunt Anna, talking with great indignation about some small-minded woman who wouldn't know an educational experience from a hole in the

ground. After that she used the same words with my father, then shut the living room door.

When I came out of school the following afternoon, I was surprised to find her waiting for me, dressed up the way she used to be when she took me to Mme Piscator. She said she had just been to see the principal and had decided to take me out for a hot chocolate on the way home, since we had to think about something very serious together right away. I felt a little scared but excited because she was talking to me as if I were suddenly all grown up about making a big choice that would affect my whole future. She had presented me with choices before about which books to take out of the library or which dress to put on. This one was about either staying at P.S. 99 or going on with my career in the theater, which would mean starting at a special school in the fall. The decision, she said, was entirely up to me.

Since it wasn't about two things I wanted equally, it didn't seem hard at all, and I wondered why she hadn't guessed the answer herself. "I want to be to be an actress," I told her.

She didn't seem to believe me. "You're absolutely sure?" she asked, so I had to say it for her all over again.

She hugged me right there in front of the girls' exit at P.S. 99 and a little later, in a drugstore on Lefferts Boulevard, allowed me to have whipped cream on my hot chocolate even though it wasn't good for my figure. She said she was proud of me for being only eight years old and understanding what was really important and that although we didn't have much money, she would see that I got my wish.

I wonder what she would have done with herself if I'd chosen P.S. 99.

On the east side of Sixty-third Street and Broadway is an empty lot that I pass quite often on the Broadway bus. A blank space like that, perfectly level and enclosed by a wire fence, is unusual in New York City. The old office building where I once went to the Professional Children's School was torn down years ago with the rest of the block, but my mind puts it back there—a brownish mass with a large square entrance and a revolving glass door leading to the tan marble lobby in which you waited for the elevator to the fourth floor. I put figures in the lobby and just outside, on Broadway, in dark coats with padded-out shoulders and the hats women used to wear in the 1940s with little spotted veils. One of them is my mother, arriving promptly just before two and waiting for me to come out, turning up her black seal collar against the cold. She is clutching her handbag and has a leatherette scrapbook under one arm that zips efficiently all around, similar to the scrapbooks carried by some of the other waiting mothers.

Most of the pages in Mother's scrapbook have yet to be filled, but the front ones contain photos of me in various outfits and poses and the precious items that document my experience so far: the playbill from *Bobino*, the *Journal-American* review, a *Bobino* photo that appeared in the *World-Telegram,* an article about me from the Kew Gardens community newspaper in which I am described as "sparkling-eyed" and "the grandchild of a man who wrote poetry." "Though an extremely gay little spirit," the reporter theorizes toward the end of her piece, "one finds a sad note in many of her recent poems," citing such lines as "Oh pretty little daffodil/What makes you full of woe?/Because upon my fairy horn/No little elf can blow" to support her psychologizing, to the great disgust of Mother and Aunt Leona. The latest addition to the scrapbook—a smiling shot of a little girl in a pinafore with the caption "Mommy! I can hear now!" from a brochure for Westinghouse hearing aids— attests to the promising start of my modeling career.

The brass elevator door opens, and I emerge in the midst of a bunch of noisy chattering children. Our impatient and freezing mothers soon close in and bear each of us separately away—to ladies' rooms in neighborhood cafeterias to have our hair recombed and our faces washed, to producers' offices or casting calls, to ballet studios or drama coaches.

Having a career as an actress seems to involve passing time in a lot of different waiting rooms, where sometimes all the seats are taken by other children and their stage mothers looking for work. They call your name, and you get about a minute in a smoky office in which to be disqualified by some grumpy middle-aged man or asked to come back and wait some more. The most important thing to remember is that honesty is not always the best policy— even if you have just turned nine, you firmly say you're eight, if that's what the script calls for, which is only a white lie, not a black one. Everything depends on type. Whenever a little blond girl is needed, you have a chance with all the other little blondes, though there are mothers of brunettes so desperate and despicable they will stoop to peroxiding their daughters' hair.

Mother has very high standards about things like that, which makes me realize how lucky I am to have her. She is appalled to think that some of my classmates at Professional Children's School are supporting entire families. Any money I make, if I ever do make any, will go into a special bank account that will be used entirely to pay for my education. Where would I be if I didn't have Mother to take me around after school because I could never break back into the theater by myself? I would be nowhere, because getting into *Bobino* was pure luck, and we can't count on having that kind of luck again.

Mother has been quick to learn the ropes. Every Tuesday afternoon we pick up *Actors Cue* on Fifty-seventh Street the moment it comes out and head for the Automat, where we can spread it out on a table and see if there's anything in it for me. I like to help do this myself, reading down the columns of casting calls on one page while Mother reads down the other. "Here's one!" I cry if my eye hits the words *girl 8–9,* and then I circle it in pencil and Mother writes down all the information. But usually all the jobs are for adults.

One day we strike gold in *Actors Cue*. It's a listing for *I Remember Mama,* a show that has just opened on Broadway and is looking for understudies, for a girl 8–9 who has to look Norwegian. Mother, who seems to know all about this show, is positive that no one could look more Norwegian than me. We rush out of the Automat and find a phone booth on Fifty-seventh Street, where Mother calls the number in the paper. "Wait till they see those braids!" she says afterward, squeezing my hands, both of us almost laughing with excitement. You read one little thing, and your mind takes off, and you can practically see yourself on the stage already right inside that glow that somehow makes you very still inside and big—that glow I want to get back to with the hushed watchers expectant in the dark.

A couple of mornings later, in the midst of a lesson on the

Puritans, the principal's secretary appears in the classroom to announce that my mother is waiting, and I pick up my books and slip
away from my desk. I've told none of the other children about the au-
dition I'm about to go to—it's what Mother and I call "a military secret." If I manage to come back after lunch in time for arithmetic, no
one will ask where I've been. At the Professional Children's School we
don't discuss business with each other—because our mothers really
can't be trusted, my mother being the notable exception.

She is waiting just outside the principal's office with some blue
velveteen hair ribbons she has just bought in Woolworth's to make
big floppy bows at the ends of my braids, which will make me look
even more Norwegian when I meet Mr. Rodgers, Mr. Hammerstein, and Mr. VanDruten, the producers and the playwright of *I
Remember Mama,* who have already seen my scrapbook. We get
into a Yellow Cab downstairs—the first taxi ride of my life—and
speed toward a theater on Forty-fifth Street, where the curtain is
up and the stage is already set like an old-fashioned kitchen for the
evening's performance. I am given a few minutes to look over a
scene where a little girl named Dagmar, who is just recovering
from an operation, returns from the hospital, pathetically asking
for her dead cat. Then I walk out onstage to show the three men in
the front row what I can do. I'm scared until I start reading, then
the scaredness becomes a funny kind of excitement propelling me
forward, while part of me hears the rise and fall and quaver of
Dagmar's voice and knows that I'm doing well.

When I return to school an hour later, I have a job in *I Remember Mama* and a few pages of typescript on onionskin paper called
"sides," containing the lines I'll have to memorize. Mother says I'm
in a hit show that will play for years and that someday the role of
Dagmar will definitely be mine, because the girl I'm understudy-

ing is sure to grow. (I'll grow too, of course, although I'm small to begin with. The question is, Which one of us will grow faster?)

In my fourth-grade class, the most successful professional child is Marty Miller, whose red hair and freckles have landed him a role

as the second youngest of twelve redheaded boys in *Life with Father;* Marty figures he's probably set for the whole run, growing out of one role every year or so and into another until his retirement around the age of twelve. Twelve, Marty Miller informs me, is when everyone's career usually ends for a while, until they get old enough to come back as adults, because teenagers, according to him, are usually played by actors in their twenties.

"But that's not fair!" I protest.

Marty shrugs. "So what? That's the way it is. You get too big, and you're finished. I don't care anyway," he says philosophically. "My uncle has everything all worked out."

When I ask him what he means, he says the two of them have a secret plan. Marty's uncle runs a furniture factory in the Bronx and has promised to save a job for him—he's looking forward to being in the furniture business for the rest of his life.

When I ask Mother if it's true that I'll be finished with the theater by the age of twelve, she sighs and says, "We'll cross that bridge when we come to it." Meanwhile she advises me not to worry about it, because I still have years in which to establish myself.

We don't go home for dinner anymore now that I have a job. It doesn't make sense to go all the way back to Kew Gardens on the subway, when I have to show up at the Music Box Theater by seven-thirty in case something bad has happened to Carolyn Hummel. For several weeks I have to watch her perform as Dagmar so I can learn all the stage business. Mother thinks Carolyn's already getting too big to play Dagmar—that she's ten if she's a day and "practically bursting out of her costumes." But night after night Carolyn goes on, giving her same phlegmatic performance, which I can soon imitate inflection by inflection. Backstage, she barely says hello to me, as if she can look into my heart and see all the jealousy I can't help feeling, my desperate hope that she'll come down with measles or chicken pox, though I'd settle for a short-term stomachache. One week in February Carolyn Hummel has such a terrible cold, I'm asked to stand by, but she performs even with laryngitis. Everyone says she's a real little trouper.

Because of our new schedule, I can no longer give my father his big hello when he comes home from work or dance for him after dinner, but he turns up two or three nights a week to join Mother and me at the Fifty-seventh Street Automat. He'll give me a fistful of nickels and send me off to look in all the little glass windows and carefully choose whatever I want to eat. I don't have to worry about my figure the way I do when I'm alone with Mother. I get fish cakes and Boston baked beans or macaroni and cheese and my favorite dessert, lemon meringue pie, while he and Mother have their few minutes alone together, talking about whatever grown-ups talk about, which mostly seems to be money or having a pain in one place or the other. After dinner my father walks us to the stage door of the Music Box Theater and kisses each of us good-bye, sometimes looking glum until he remembers to smile, then he travels back to Kew Gardens for an evening with the sports section. Mother says she hopes one day we'll have a normal life again, as if it's all out of her hands. But a normal life would mean that I wouldn't be in show business, and neither of us wants that now that I'm off to such a good start.

Except for Mme Piscator, I liked it better being in *Bobino*. When I was Cupid, I was somehow part of everything; here I always feel out on the periphery—not the genuine Dagmar, just an impostor. I feel shy and embarrassed as I check in with the stage manager just as all the real actors are hurrying in to put on their makeup and costumes. They go importantly upstairs to their dressing rooms while I perform my only other official duty, stopping in at the prop room to visit the two black-and-white cats that are used in the production so we won't be strangers to each other if I ever get to carry them onstage. They're tuxedo cats with identical black-and-white markings, but their personalities are entirely different. The one that appears with Carolyn throughout the first act looks asleep even when it's supposed to be acting and barely twitches a whisker when I lift it out of its cage. The one I think of as the understudy cat is always pacing and meowing and looking for a clever way to escape. It's only used for a minute in Act Two, when it can be absolutely counted upon to swish its tail back and forth from under a blanket to prove that it's still alive. The understudy cat greets me with frantic enthusiasm. If I ever get to play Dagmar, I'll give it its big break.

Since there's no room for us backstage, Mother and I spend the entire performance in the Music Box smoking lounge, where members of the audience sometimes stare at me during intermission, as if they can't imagine what a child is doing up so late. It never dawns on them that I too belong to the play they've been watching. When I'm not upstairs watching Carolyn Hummel, I read or do my homework or put different costumes on the Storybook Dolls that I carry around in the red hatbox that also contains my makeup.

Two other understudies, Len Metz and George Dill, are also killing time in the lounge. They're middle-aged and smoke cigars like my father, but they're not gentlemen about it; when Mother puts down her knitting to wave away the fumes, they don't take the hint. Sometimes they give me lessons in gin rummy. Len has a beautiful British accent and looks a little like James Mason—he used to do Shakespeare in London; George, who is very tall and has a true Norwegian look, has played many leading roles in summer stock. They both predict *I Remember Mama* will run on Broadway forever like *Life with Father*. There's nothing like a steady income, George Dill assures me, trying to make me feel better about Carolyn Hummel's continuing state of good health. Len Metz advises me to fight boredom by reading my way through Charles Dickens—for Christmas he gives me a copy of *David Copperfield* with a personal inscription.

My other new acquaintance, Sue Riley, the ladies' room attendant, is an even older person. Under a hairnet that knots in the center of her forehead, she has flaming red hair, which Mother says is dyed; she lives in a rooming house where she has to fight with people about getting more space in the Frigidaire. She drives Mother crazy because she talks too much, but I like to hear about the days when Sue had a perfect figure and danced in the Ziegfeld Follies and got flowers from Mr. Ziegfeld; after that she swam around for years in a glass tank at something called the Hippodrome. "Want to see a good pair of legs?" she says one night, hiking up the skirt of her black uniform so Len and George can have a look. "*Ex*-quisite!" Len says in his Shakespearean voice, as Mother catches my eye and shakes her head. Sue never explains how she fell to her present career of wiping sinks and handing out towels. But since her favorite expression is "It's not what you know but who you know," you can only conclude that she didn't get to meet the right people.

By the end of Act Two, I'm very sleepy, but understudies don't have to wait for the curtain calls. George and Len put away their cards and head for a tavern on Eighth Avenue in their fedoras and camel overcoats. Mother and I hurry to the subway through the Great White Way, which is dim and gray with all the neon signs off because of the war. Often we have to push through oncoming waves of soldiers and sailors looking for a good time before going overseas to fight the enemy. The servicemen who get free tickets to see *I Remember Mama* are very polite and laugh harder and clap more than anyone else. But sometimes a drunken soldier in Times Square will make the great mistake of whistling at Mother, and she'll put on a stern expression and grab me by the elbow to rush me along and warn me not to turn my head. On Forty-second Street the air smells of hot dogs and beer, and there are crowds in the cafeterias and friendly young women with dark lipstick and long fingernails and very high heels saying "Hello there!" to strangers from doorways and the movies play all night despite the dark marquees. It's always very late by the time we descend into the subway to go home—late enough for the old man who sells flowers in the Forty-second Street station to start making rosebuds out of yesterday's roses, plucking the faded petals off and throwing them away.

At some point during my first year as an understudy, my father's face lost the last of its boyishness and took on a pinched look. Whenever we were home with him, he seemed to lie down an awful lot. At first my mother said it was indigestion—now that we had to eat out so much, he missed her home cooking. Then she told me he had an ulcer, something grown-ups got when they worried, though she didn't say what could be worrying my father enough to make him sick. It never occurred to me that it might have something to do with our new way of life—with my acting career, which had brought about my mother's absence from the household. My father had always approved of everything Mother did; the idea that they were happy together, an ideal married couple, had been drummed into me—the proof was, they never had arguments. What was happiness for grown-ups, anyway? Until I was in my teens and began wondering about sex, I had no curiosity about my parents' sleeping arrangements—those two chaste beds tightly covered by beige chenille bedspreads. The gap between them, as far as I knew, was never crossed in the middle of the night, though when I was very little, I'd sometimes found them sitting up in the same bed sharing the newspaper on Sunday mornings, looking rather pleased with each other.

Every Sunday, when the Music Box was closed, we had our weekly opportunity to be normal. My parents would sleep late in their separate beds until my father got up to make oatmeal in the pressure cooker to give my mother a break. Mother was fond of newfangled devices that brought an element of novelty into the kitchen—she had bought one of the original Waring blenders and for the first few months blended everything in sight, inventing banana milk and several imaginative kinds of whipped Jell-O. She soon achieved control of the temperamental pressure cooker, but my father did not—every few Sundays there would be a hiss and a loud pop, the oatmeal would land on the kitchen ceiling, and he would have to sheepishly mop it off. The pressure cooker had arrived with my father's ulcer and had become my mother's chief means of working toward a cure, preparing the "pure" and utterly bland meals the three of us would eat together at home from then on, as if the absence of flavor in my father's life, due to his mysterious worries, was something we all had to share.

It's hard for me to think of him on Sundays without the radio playing in the background. But for my father, stretched out on the living room couch, the radio increasingly became foreground—first the morning news about the war, then the noonday opera program with Milton Cross, then the ball game droning in from somewhere, the oceanic roars of the crowds, the hits, the strikes, the fly balls that seemed to mesmerize him and put him beyond my reach, as if he'd discovered the ability to disappear in plain sight.

Once when I went into the kitchen for a glass of milk, I heard my mother talking bitterly on the phone about some man who had his mind on chasing balls instead of getting somewhere.

"Who is that?" I asked her.

"No one you know," she said quickly. "Isn't it possible to have some privacy around here, young lady?"

After watching many performances of *I Remember Mama,* I decided to write plays myself. They seemed easy because you didn't have to find ways of making the lines rhyme. Characters could say ordinary things like "Hello" and "What do you mean?" and "Where's Father?" which I found a great relief.

The Father character in most of my plays was a fragile but lovable man who got into trouble. He'd lose his job and end up in debtors' prison or rashly give all his money away and have nothing left to buy his children presents. The children—a boy and a girl—would have to save the day with some additional assistance from fairies. "Never mind, Father," they'd say consolingly at the end of Act One when things always looked darkest. The Mother character had very few lines and hardly appeared onstage at all.

One of my first efforts, *Patience's Christmas,* became the fourth grade's contribution to the Christmas assembly. I not only directed it but felt entitled to play the leading role of Patience. Since my classmates were all professionals, no one accused me of being stuck-up. Marty Miller volunteered to play Father because he was sick of playing kids. An elfin-looking redhead named Mitzi with experience in her parents' nightclub act was the Fairy Queen—at one of our school assemblies, Mitzi had appeared onstage in a pink-sequined leotard and given a memorable rendition of "My Heart Belongs to Daddy," after a series of cartwheels and headstands. I incorporated the glittering leotard and the cartwheels into *Patience's Christmas.* At rehearsals we all giggled a lot and sometimes got a little wild because we were unaccustomed to acting in amateur productions. The boys especially would forget themselves and start throwing erasers and chalk at each other, and I'd sometimes have to remind the cast that we were actually engaged in serious business. "Children, ve must vork, vork, vork," I couldn't resist saying once or twice, stamping my foot à la Mme Piscator.

My play had an elaborate finale—a rousing song-and-dance number called "Happiness" performed by the entire cast. The lyrics—in my usual vein—were about loving the birds and bees and flowers and trees: "If we can love these things/Why can't you?/But the time is getting late/And so adieu." Since my characters happened to be Norwegian, these words were sung to the tune of Grieg's "Norwegian Dance," which was played on the violin by a cherubic, mischievous fiddler named Michael Rabin, who was said to be a child prodigy. (By sixth grade, my friend Michael would disappear from our midst forever, so that he would have more time to practice without wasting so much of his day among kids. After a remarkable career, cut short by nervous breakdowns, he died in his early thirties, a burntout case.)

Mother, of course, attended the performance of my play; afterward she came up to embrace me, radiating excitement, predicting I'd grow up to be another Rodgers and Hammerstein, as if suddenly that would be an even better idea than acting. Didn't I want to learn to write my own music? she kept asking, though Edvard Grieg had been good enough for me. I'd come up with that song just because I needed one, not thinking it was a trick I'd be obliged to repeat. But Mother was greedy when it came to my talents. Whatever I did, she had to wring out more. The play had been mine, but after she started talking about it to everyone she knew, it somehow became hers, and I no longer cared about it.

Soon she started looking around for the perfect music teacher to develop my creativity. Fortunately, it took her quite a while to find one. I was already busy enough after school. Although it was clear by now that I would never be a dancer, I was going to ballet three times a week and was even wobbling around in toe shoes. When Mother heard that something called toetap was going to sweep Broadway, I had lessons in that too for a while in special shoes from Capezio's, but it never caught on. In addition, there were the expensive sessions with my private acting coach, Irene Beck, in a dark apartment with very dirty windows across the street from the Hotel Wellington, where Mother had once studied at the Ziegler Academy of Normal Singing—oddly enough, she never called my attention to that address or told me why it had once been important to her.

Miss Beck was a tiny woman with a powerful voice that emanated from her diaphragm, even though she was almost doubled over with arthritis. She had a darkly handsome, much younger husband who collected the dollar bills Mother took from her handbag—Mother suspected him of being "no good." One afternoon a week, Miss Beck improved my diction with diagrams showing me where to put my tongue; then I learned various dialects—French, Irish, Cockney, southern—none of which I ever had occasion to use, though I can still do a speech from the long-forgotten Broadway hit *Peg o' My Heart:* "Oy'll be missin' ye tirrible, Father darlin' . . . ," with the rolling *r*'s Miss Beck taught me.

As far as my acting was concerned, Miss Beck, a passionate devotée of the Stanislavski System, had the single aim of teaching me to be "natural"; somehow being natural was really the most difficult thing in the world. It seemed to be something I had once known and then forgotten due to my previous training with Mme Piscator. At times Miss Beck would make me sit still for nearly half an hour working on my concentration; I would concentrate on being a flower in need of water or a lazy cat on a summer afternoon. Mother began to say we were throwing out money.

By the summer Miss Beck had been replaced. My new acting coach drilled me in scenes from Broadway plays that could be used in auditions, making me copy each of her gestures and intonations.

Although I never saw Miss Beck again, I remained under the influence of her teachings. When I learned that Carolyn Hummel was going away to camp for the month of July and that I would be playing Dagmar, I decided to make my performance absolutely natural, but didn't put my ideas into practice until after I had been onstage for several nights. There was a long scene at the end of Act One of *I Remember Mama,* where Mama and her family gathered around a table to listen to the old man who boarded with them read *The Hound of the Baskervilles.* The lights would slowly dim, with everyone sitting very still and a single spotlight on Mady Christians, who played Mama, entranced by the reading, with her arm around Dagmar. I did not think a real child would sit still for such a long time; a real child would be a little restless in her seat even if she was enjoying the story she was hearing; she might even yawn a bit if she was up past her bedtime.

I thought everyone would be very pleased with my realistic touches and would see how much they added to the performance. But the night I tried them out, Mady Christians grabbed me the moment the curtain went down. Towering above me, her face flushed with rage beneath her golden coronet of Norwegian braids, she shook me by the shoulders, screaming, "You little monkey!"—a performance quite unlike her portrayal of the saintly matriarch I had watched her play night after night. Barely able to speak, I tried to explain that I had only meant to be natural, but she accused me of deliberately trying to upstage her and warned me that I must never dare do so again. Another actor tried to make me feel better by saying Mady Christians was really a bitch, especially when she'd had a few too many. A few too many what? I wondered. And what was a bitch? When I later asked Mother, she

said it was a word I must never use; it went on a list of other forbidden words I'd heard around the theater.

Another of my innovations—the debut in Act One of the understudy cat—also proved a disaster. On the cat's first appearance under the brilliant stage lights without its head covered, it had clung to me, paralyzed by stage fright, but had otherwise seemed professional. The second night it started clawing the air soon after we made our entrance. When I sat down with it on a bench in Mama's kitchen in front of a table loaded with blue-and-white coffee cups, it lunged at the red-and-white-checked tablecloth beneath them and wouldn't let go. Mady Christians and two other

members of the cast rushed over to save the china by resting their
elbows on the table as uneasy ripples of laughter rose from the audience. Meanwhile, like living embodiments of the precept "The
show must go on," we all continued to say our lines as though
nothing unusual were happening; I even still managed to coo en-
dearments at the frantic animal. With one desperate yank, I finally
extricated its claws from the tablecloth; a moment later Mady
Christians delivered my exit cue sternly and several minutes ahead
of time. Mortified but grateful, I rushed my fellow understudy
offstage.

For the rest of my run, Miss Christians would neither speak to
me nor look at me backstage, though she still had to put her arm
around me at the conclusion of Act One and when I came home
from the hospital in Act Two. That was the scene I always looked
forward to particularly. Wrapped in a fireproof quilt, I was carried
across the stage by Marlon Brando, who played my older brother
Nels and who I'd recently realized was tremendously handsome.
He remembered me from *Bobino* and treated me like a real kid sister, teasing me about a mouse that he swore had taken up resi-
dence on the set or feeding me ice from the water cooler backstage.
"Okay, kid," he'd whisper, trying to crack me up just before our
entrance, "Tonight I'm gonna drop ya."

Once I'd lived down my mistakes, I would have been happy to
play Dagmar forever, but Carolyn Hummel came back from
camp, and by August everything was the same again, except that
now there were often nights when I wished I didn't have to go to
the Music Box to sit in the lounge. Mother was even more disappointed. She had convinced herself and told everyone I'd surely be
discovered and had even printed up cards with my picture on them
and dropped them off with agents and producers, who might be

interested in coming to see me act. But all I had to show for my four weeks onstage was a cast photo in the *Herald Tribune* and my name in the playbill with a paragraph that said my favorite book was *Uncle Tom's Cabin* and that I was interested in playing Little Eva, which wasn't even exactly true.

With school still closed and no one to play with during my long days in Kew Gardens, I drove Mother crazy by begging her to let me have a kitten. She insisted it would make too much work for her, but for some reason I wanted a kitten more than I'd ever wanted anything. Why couldn't I have one if I always did everything she wanted? Why did she care more about scratches on her furniture than about me?

I'll always remember a walk with my father on one of those long, tense Sundays when I didn't have to go to the theater. Where that Sunday falls chronologically, I have no precise idea, but it must have been before my tenth birthday, before we moved out of the apartment in Kew Gardens and into the one in Upper Manhattan near Columbia University where I would live until July 4, 1955, when I left home at nineteen for a room I'd secretly rented in the neighborhood, with my books and clothes stuffed into a shopping cart.

From the time I was four or five, I'd often played with the idea of running away. The thought would usually come to me when Mother sent me downstairs to wait for her. How easy it would be to slip away, to not be there by the time she got out of the elevator, though where to go seemed an unanswerable question. I remember trying to calculate how much money I'd need to disappear successfully—at least two dollars, maybe as much as five. And how would I ever get that? I wondered. I tended to be a cautious child, not given to rash actions. At school, I was considered such a model of sensible behavior that a bad boy was forced to sit next to me after the teacher had separated him from his riotous companions. "Are you a good girl?" he'd sometimes ask me contemptuously, and I'd reluctantly answer that I supposed I was. Since for years I lacked a best friend, I never tried my lawless thoughts out on anyone. But on that walk with my father, I made the mistake of revealing what I was thinking.

He'd asked me to come out with him late in the afternoon while my mother began preparations for dinner. He'd smoked his cigar, and I'd chattered away, holding his hand, thrilled to have him to myself. We'd walked for blocks, all the way to the edge of another neighborhood. When we had to turn back because my mother would start wondering what had happened to us, I didn't want to go home. Not yet, at any rate—maybe never. The feeling that had come over me was so strong, I was powerless to stop myself from saying what I already knew I shouldn't: "Let's you and me run away together, Dad."

Looking down at me in affectionate disbelief, not reproachful yet, my father asked me what kind of nonsense I was saying.

With my heart in my mouth, I repeated the suggestion. "Let's you and me run away together, Dad."

"Without your *mother?*"

I knew there was still time to take it back, to say I was just kidding, but all I could do was to hang my head.

My father raised his voice as he never had before. "I never want to hear you say anything like that again! Do you hear me!" I clutched at his hand, but he pulled it back and started walking away from me at a brisk pace, as if he would just as soon never set eyes on me again. I trailed after him disconsolately for blocks, lying to him the rest of the way home.

"I didn't mean it! I didn't mean it!"

Whether or not I actually convinced him, my father seemed to forgive me. Before we went upstairs, he wiped my face with his handkerchief and told me he'd say nothing to Mother because it would hurt her far too much. But he never asked me what was wrong, or realized that the job of being the one who made Mother happy was becoming too much for me.

I'd begun to be more and more aware that my mother wanted to have me all to herself and to keep me separate from any influence that might take me away from her. Even after we moved into the city, she was reluctant to let me visit the girls I knew at school or have them over to our apartment. Those girls, she said, were a waste of time, and I'd only pick up their bad habits. If I wasted my time now, she warned, I'd never amount to anything. By my second year in *I Remember Mama,* she demanded more from me than ever. The two of us seemed to be working frantically against a deadline: If I wasn't famous by the age of eighteen, I would never be famous at all.

I remember feeling astonished when Mother unexpectedly made a friend of her own. Evelyn Starr was an unmarried, enthusiastic woman with a southern accent who worked for a realty company on the Upper West Side and had gone to great lengths to help Mother find our new apartment. She was thrilled by Mother's connection to the Broadway theater and thought we were a very remarkable family. For a while whenever the phone rang, Mother would say, "It must be Evelyn Starr again," and look very pleased as she complained of being besieged by Evelyn's calls and invitations. "Are you going to have lunch with Miss Starr today?" I'd ask hopefully as I set out for school.

Evelyn Starr worked in a ground-floor office on Seventy-second Street. You could look in and see her at the front desk, typing or chattering on the phone, wearing one of the navy blue suits she said she got on sale for practically nothing at Saks Fifth Avenue. You could even catch a glimpse of Mother's friend from the Number 5 bus after it turned off Broadway, and I'd always remember to look out the window just in time to make sure she was still there. If Mother had Evelyn, maybe I'd be allowed to have a friend myself.

Our move into the city made it quite easy for me to disappear, should I ever get up the nerve to do so, because I was now allowed to ride back and forth to school by myself on the Broadway trolley. Without anyone being the wiser, I could get off, if I really wanted to, at any stop along the way or even at the end of the line on Forty-second Street. The same nickel would get me on the forbidden subway. Suddenly Mother claimed it was dangerous, though she and I had been riding it together for years.

One morning I decided to go to school by the IRT, just to see what would happen. Looking over my shoulder to make sure I was unobserved, I sneaked down the steps of the 116th Street station. To my horror, when I reached the platform, an old lady who lived in our building and who often had elevator conversations with Mother called out my name in surprise and insisted on knowing where I was going. Thinking quickly, I said, "I'm *not* Joyce," in the nastiest tone I could summon up. "You're not?" she said in bewilderment. "But you look just like her." "Listen, lady," I said. "I know that girl Joyce, and I hate her. If she ever bothers me, I'm going to beat her up." Looking truly aghast, the old lady backed away. Still in my new persona, I marched to the end of the platform, swinging my books by their strap, and waited there alone for my train. It was satisfying to hear a few days later from Mother about some dreadful girl, probably a juvenile delinquent, who evidently knew me and was jealous because I was in the theater and whom I must never speak to again.

* * *

When I was ten and a half, *I Remember Mama* closed on Broadway, and Rodgers and Hammerstein did not invite me to play Dagmar on the road. Carolyn Hummel wasn't invited either—they'd found a new Dagmar, younger and smaller than either of us. I could no longer be mistaken for an eight-year-old; my chest was beginning to get hilly, and a few hairs that Mother said were nothing had sprouted under my arms. By the summer, instead of reporting to the Music Box Theater, I went to the Unemployment Insurance Office. There I was unquestionably the shortest person on line and attracted a good deal of embarrassing attention.

Call *REGISTRY* For

**JOYCE ALICE ROSS**

**VOICE RANGE:** 4-14 yrs.
**ACTUAL AGE:** 10 yrs.
**TYPE OF WORK:** Straight, sensitive, brats, comedy. Any type of little girl.
**DIALECTS:** French, Italian, Southern, German, Russian, Irish, Scotch, Norwegian, Negro.
**THEATRE:** B'way: Current — "I Remember Mama". "Bobino".
**RADIO:** WNYC.

LA 4-1200
Ac 2-5299

620 W. 116 St., N.Y.C.

Mother said I was in the awkward age and thought radio might be the answer. I made up some monologues to show off my repertoire of dialects, and we went on a round of auditions at advertising agencies and on different floors of the RCA building. The end result was two lines in a commercial. *Teacher: Class, what ocean borders Peru? Child: The Atlantic! Teacher: Wrong. Child: The Pacific! Teacher: Right! That little girl eats Wheaties!* Mother said it was a foot in the door.

Her latest plan was to turn me into a *Wunderkind* creator of Broadway musicals. She had truly convinced herself that with the right training I could blossom into a kind of Rodgers and Hammerstein combined, apparently forgetting that the catchy tune in my fourth-grade play had originated with Edvard Grieg. Mother had searched all over Queens for the perfect music teacher and found one in a neighborhood near Kew Gardens just before we moved. From that time on, even after I became unemployed and we had to borrow money for my private lessons from Aunt Anna, I spent one hour with James Bleecker, a patrician, silver-haired gentleman, every Saturday morning, with Mother sitting in a corner of the studio pretending to read a magazine as she hungrily absorbed every word that dropped from my music teacher's lips. She had freely criticized Mme Piscator and Irene Beck, but in Mr. Bleecker's presence Mother became bashful and reverential as she inquired about my progress or asked how many hours I should be devoting to my music for maximum results. Mr. Bleecker must have seemed to her the embodiment of all that was classical.

He had developed a following through teaching piano and composition simultaneously, and his other students were considerably older than I was. A mild-mannered man, he had a vein of sour grapes that surfaced whenever he discussed the sad state of contemporary music. He warned all his students against venturing into atonality, and I remember his utter contempt for a young upstart named John Cage, who he claimed played the piano with his elbow. "How awful!" Mother said, shocked to think that such liberties could be taken.

When I was much younger, I had sometimes experimented with Mother's baby grand—banging on its keys or strumming its strings like a harpist or making small objects vanish behind the keyboard into what I thought of as Pianoland. Once a visiting

piano tuner had thrilled me by retrieving from the depths of the
George Steck several pennies and a little silver locket turned completely black. But I'd never yearned to do any actual piano playing
myself. I'd been quite happy to leave all that to Mother. Now that
I'd been pushed into her realm, I could not make myself comfortable there. Music, unlike language or theater, felt like alien territory. Still, until I was almost grown up, there was no escape from
Mother's strange determination to have me become a famous
woman composer.

Our visits to Mr. Bleecker continued for the next seven years,
ending only when I entered Barnard College, across the street from
our apartment, where I had to placate Mother by immediately en-
rolling in a course in counterpoint. Eventually I had learned to get
through "Für Elise" or the "Moonlight Sonata" without too many
mistakes, but I never managed to play as though my heart was in
it. Nor did I ever feel proud of the melodies I ground out at
Mother's baby grand, always aware that she was listening in the
background to see if I had come up with anything. Mr. Bleecker,
too much of a gentleman to bring my mother to her senses, never
told her that I had no real gift. But the more I learned about
music, the more I suspected the truth. Was it right that I could
make up song lyrics easily enough but never hear in my head the
music that would accompany them or that I could only find tunes
on the piano by trial and error? Would a real composer work that
way? I wondered. But with Mother sitting right there during my
lessons, I never had the courage to raise such questions.

During high school, I fended Mother off by writing three full-
length musical comedies, which she actually tried to get produced.
One of them she sent to Rodgers and Hammerstein, who never
wrote back. I would have died rather than show them to any of
the bohemian folksinging friends I secretly hung out with on

weekends in Greenwich Village. The musical comedies belonged to Mother, not to me.

I finally quit music during my senior year at Barnard shortly after Mother had made me begin taking private lessons in orchestration with Wallingford Reigger, a more honest teacher than Mr. Bleecker as well as the first true artist I'd ever known. After I tried to explain to Mother how mortified I'd felt going through the motions of writing scores, she wrapped my musicals up in plastic along with all my other compositions and put them away in the locked drawer at the top of her bureau. By the time I found them there four decades later, I was incapable of playing them. I had never touched the piano again.

When my mother died, I inherited the George Steck baby grand— the mahogany repository of her frustrated longings and my old tormentor. I did not want it, yet felt I could not let go of it. I'd lie awake at night mentally rearranging the furniture in my living room so that I could make room for the piano, but I could never find the right place for it.

At an antiques fair that spring, I met a Russian dealer who specialized in old pianos. I asked him to come and look at the Steck, knowing that I needed to assess its value. He told me the sounding board was cracked in four places and that it would cost thousands to fix. He offered to give me three hundred dollars for the instrument and arrange to have it taken away. I accepted, and my sleepless nights ended. When the check bounced, I laughed.

Just before I quit music, I'd been been cutting classes to work on a story that had suddenly opened up to me the way I knew I wanted to write. "The End of the Beach" was not perfect, but it was as true to my memories of certain feelings as I could make it, and I could see how its truth had somehow charged its language. I realized I'd never feel the same certainty about any of my musical compositions.

That fall, I'd turned nineteen. Far from dedicating myself to becoming famous, I was floundering in the deep waters of a love affair with a thirty-year-old instructor at Barnard, a magnetic, troubled man with a limp and a wandering eye, in the midst of a divorce. At the time this affair—complicated by the fact that I was still living at home under Mother's surveillance—seemed the most important thing that had ever happened to me. But now I think the story that so insistently demanded to be written had even more impact upon my life.

Under no circumstances could it have been shown to my mother, for it was as much about her as it was about me. Putting it on paper had the feeling of an illicit but necessary act, requiring steely ruthlessness. That spring, when "The End of the Beach" was published in the Barnard literary magazine, I hid the two copies they gave me with a friend and never brought them home. I could neither stop myself from writing about Mother nor stop protecting her from the discovery of who I was and how I felt— as if she might crumble if she ever knew I'd pulled up the blinds and exposed so much to light. Perhaps my mother was—and remains—my muse. My negative muse, if that makes any sense.

The beach where the family I wrote about quietly ruptures during an extended summer vacation "when nothing ever seemed to happen" was the one in Montauk, where my parents rented a bungalow for two interminable months after I graduated from the Professional Children's School and retired from the theater. In the fall I would be going to an all-girls public high school, where I was going to be a year younger than the rest of my class because Mother had made me skip seventh grade. She seemed to be trying to rush me through what remained of my childhood—to get it out of the way so that she and I could go on to greater things—while simultaneously attempting to keep me a little girl as long as possible. For the moment, I was supposed to embrace the opportunity to be "normal" though "normal" seemed a great comedown to me after my years as a professional child. Already I was thinking how I could get back into the theater by saving up my allowance to buy *Actors Cue* and showing up at auditions on my own.

At twelve and a half, I couldn't help feeling all washed up. But Mother's sense of anticlimax must have been even more devastating. Her role as my impresario had given her an outlet for her ambition, ingenuity, and restlessness that had almost been enough for her. Now it was back to the vacuum and the pressure cooker, to the grind of keeping up appearances on the twenty-five dollars a week my father gave her for household expenses. Other men had risen

after the war, but he was still an auditor at the Metropolitan Tobacco Company and showed no inclination to better his position.

Just before we left New York for the summer, my mother went
to the hospital for a mysterious operation, which was probably a
hysterectomy. The bungalow had been rented so that she could re-

cuperate by the sea. We didn't know a soul in Montauk, and we
didn't have a car. We walked back and forth from the house to the
general store, from the house to the beach over low dunes covered
with bayberry, scrub pine, and blackberry briars. I had never been
taught to swim, on the theory that I might drown, and I felt too
old to make sand castles, so the beach soon became boring to me
with its rituals of spreading out the blanket, putting up the um-

brella, letting Mother smear me with suntan oil, collecting shells and stones. When I looked around, I saw no one even approximately my age on the sparsely populated sand. Day after day, Mother and I were alone, although on weekends we'd be joined by my father.

Our isolation also wore upon Mother. After a couple of weeks she began talking to me in a way she'd never talked before, telling me things I did not want to know but could not avoid taking in. I'd once read a Hans Christian Andersen story in which a girl gets a piece of glass in her eye, and after that everything looks ugly to her because she can only see its imperfections. I began to feel like that girl.

"The flies were always with them," I would write seven years later, "huge horseflies that seemed to be indestructible. The sound they made merged with the drone of the baseball game on the radio and the slap of the waves on the beach. One sound cancelled another . . . and by the middle of the summer, there was only a vast silence. Her mother's voice became part of the silence, too."

In our revolving conversations, my mother decimated articles of faith I'd never really questioned up till then. I'd been brought up to believe that my parents—two smallish, round-faced people who could have been "brother and sister," who never yelled or argued or even disagreed in my presence—were content with one another. We didn't have money, I'd often been told, but we had something infinitely more important—a happy family. Even when I'd been very lonely myself, even when I'd tried to get my father to run away with me, I'd believed my mother and father were perfectly matched, that they loved each other in the mild, unecstatic way married couples were supposed to, though if I'd been asked to think about it, I would probably have said that my father was the one who loved more.

But my mother that summer had far too much empty time in which to take stock of what her life had come to. She looked at herself and saw a forty-five-year-old woman with lines on her face and graying hair; she looked at my father and saw someone the world would consider a nobody, a husband who had failed to give her what

she wanted; she looked at me and saw a child turning into a teenager, a girl who might become boy crazy any minute and at some point in the future rebellious enough to leave her. Although I hadn't even thought about dating and was being sent to a school where I was guaranteed to meet no boys, she lectured me on deferring marriage until I was "established," or in other words, extremely old.

"Don't ever marry a man who has his mind on chasing balls," she'd warn me in a low voice as we sat on the cramped porch, away from my father listening to the Dodgers play the Yankees in the bedroom. "Don't make the same mistakes I did. I won't let you." If it were not for her marriage, I was given to understand, and the responsibility of raising me, she might even now be performing Schubert on the concert stage, though of course the Depression had also put an end to her dreams. Perhaps because it seemed less unbearable than acknowledging her own failure of will, the limitations of her talent, the way my grandfather's suicide had stunted the lives of his daughters, this was the version of her story she had chosen to believe.

"Twenty years on the same job!" Marion, the frustrated wife in my story, exclaims bitterly to her daughter Susan. "I used to think he could get somewhere if I pushed him a little."

"Susan realized," I wrote, "that she and her mother were playing a game. They never mentioned it or set down rules for it, but it was a game nevertheless. The object was to watch for her father to make some foolish slip and to smile a furtive, knowing smile at each other, when he was caught. It was a strangely exciting game. At first, Susan wondered if it were wrong, but then she decided it couldn't be, since her mother was playing it too."

My mother must have desperately needed to talk to someone that summer. But she had far too much pride to reveal her misery to a mere acquaintance like Evelyn Starr or to her unmarried sisters, who thought she had been pretty lucky compared to them. She must have hoped that what she revealed to me would have the effect of binding me to her the way Anna and Leona were bound to my grandmother. But perhaps, in her pain, she didn't quite know what she was doing and made the classic mistake of thinking that a child, half-unconscious, would be a neutral kind of listening post.

When I read the story now, it's hard to separate the fictional heightening in it from what I actually remember. The portrait of "Marion," as I called the mother, seems too unshaded—by systematically belittling the father, insisting their daughter see him as an inept clown, she deliberately tries to destroy the child's relationship with him. I no longer am sure that was my mother's actual intent. I have to remind myself that at nineteen I was still too much in her power to forgive her for her desperation, her terrifying need to live through me because she had never managed to live for herself.

Still, the consequences for the child in the story are true to my memory of them. By the end of that summer, my mother had lost me. I couldn't forgive her for what she'd said about my father. I couldn't forgive myself for betraying him by listening, and so I lost him too.

The bleakest moment in the story I wrote comes when Susan's father approaches her and suggests they play a game of catch. As her mother watches from under the striped umbrella, the little girl stares at him with ruthless objectivity "as though she had never seen him before. . . . He was shivering a little, with the cold touch of the sea still wet on his body. His eyes blinked helplessly in the sunlight. . . . 'He looks like a pudding, a silly old pudding,' Susan thought. 'Like butterscotch pudding when you take it out of the icebox and it starts to melt.' " Just as I did, Susan abruptly turns from her father and mother and takes off.

I remember that walk in the wet sand along the Montauk shoreline to this day—the feeling that if I kept at it long enough, one foot leaving its imprint in front of the other, I would come to the end of the beach and find myself back in the city. I wanted to be in a place full of other people, where I could let go of my new way of seeing. But finally I sank down on the sand because I was tired and only twelve and a half and waited for someone to come and get me. A dot approached me from the distance; gradually the dot turned into my father.

Someday I was really going to do it, I thought, get away from them. And then, I expected to be happy for the rest of my life.

# TWO

# Red, White, and Black

*One night, thirty-eight years after I wait for him on a sidewalk in Manhattan and he fails to arrive, the phone rings. The call is from a woman with a slight southern accent, the mechanical intonation of a telemarketer: "May I speak to Mr. Jim Johnson?"*

*My heart plummets toward my belly, a million images, unleashed, whirl through my head.*

*But it's only a minor coincidence, a computer error somewhere out in cyberspace.*

*So I manage to say very coldly and sternly before putting down the receiver, "There is no Jim Johnson here."*

The first time I saw him, no one knew his name. It was at a party at the end of winter in 1962. I think we were celebrating Verta Mae Grosvenor's imminent divorce, though her invitations had promised that, according to Nostradamus, the world would end that particular Saturday night. Verta was famous in the downtown art world for her parties. By midnight her walk-up was full of wine and smoke, the windowpanes were sweating from steam, from the accumulated breath of the swaying, bobbing crowd—painters and their women, mostly, who had come up from the Village, emptying out the Cedar Bar. I knew everyone in the room and a couple of them too well, and I leaned against a wall in the slithery blue dress I'd bought earlier that day at Klein's and wished I hadn't come as I watched the dancing couples gyrate their hips at each other in the energetic new fashion while the hi-fi blasted a Chubby Checker 45.

I suddenly heard, "Why do you hang back?" A serious question addressed to me. I looked up into the face of a stranger with fierce blue eyes and thick brown hair who seemed to have recognized something I hadn't intended to reveal about myself. He delivered those five unsettling words, then veered away through the crowd. By the time I collected myself and looked for him, he was gone. Who *was* that? I asked a couple of people.

Over the next few days he kept cropping up in my path. I'd glimpse him from various distances, close and far—he'd be turning a corner on St. Marks Place or on the other side of Eighth Street, walking very fast in the heavy gray sweater he'd worn to the party, a brown-and-red scarf wound around his neck, his shoulders hunched against the cold—Why didn't he have a coat? I wondered. Once as I sat in Rappaport's Dairy Restaurant on Second Avenue drinking coffee at six A.M. I saw him go straight past, close enough to touch but on the other side of the glass.

We used to read our getting together backward, the way you read certain accidents that in retrospect seem meant to have happened. We'd examine all the elements, conjecturing how different the outcome might have been if one or two had been subtracted—if I'd stayed home that Saturday night, if his friend Ron Gorchov hadn't given him Verta's address. Maybe he'd still be alive if he'd never run into me.

He used to have a theory that our paths had crossed when he was a nineteen-year-old sailor, roaming Times Square in those crowds of servicemen Mother and I would walk through as we made our way from the Music Box Theater to the subway. He could have seen a little girl with long blond braids and wondered what she was doing out so late. "I'd have noticed *you*," he said.

The knowledge he'd brought home from the war—the fatefulness of time and place—preoccupied him. On a minesweeper during the invasion of Anzio, under continuous shelling, men had fallen all around him; he'd never understood why he'd been the one left standing. The difference between life and death, he often reminded me, could hang on a few inches. I'd resist that awareness—I wanted to believe that together we'd be safe. Yet he was not the first man I'd loved who had a piercing sense of mortality. Four years earlier, there had been Jack Kerouac, who used to try to convince me that birth equaled death, that nothing mattered because we were all headed for the Void. For Jim, everything mattered—in some ways, mattered too much.

A week before Verta's party, he'd gone out drinking, as he often did on the long empty nights in Painesville, Ohio, after his marriage had gone cold. He'd visited a feckless couple of his acquaintance who had bought a couple of his paintings; afterward they'd watched with amusement as he staggered across their snowy driveway to his car. He was halfway home when the Volvo hit a patch of ice—either that, or he'd blacked out for a moment. The next thing he knew, everything was spinning. He'd folded his arms and put his head down on them, awaiting the plunge downward into the woods. Instead the car seemed to spin itself out, coming to a dead stop in the middle of the road. He drove the last few miles very slowly, then stayed up the rest of the night drinking black coffee. The following morning he put his car keys and bank book on the kitchen table where his wife would find them, took a taxi to the Greyhound bus station, and bought a one-way ticket. "I knew I had to change everything or die," he'd later say to me.

I was twenty-six that winter and about to give up on New York. Before, I'd always been too broke to travel. After knowing Kerouac, I had little faith in movement for its own sake as any kind of solution, but I had the five hundred dollars I'd received in January when my first novel was published and no good reason to stick around. All I had to lose was the small apartment that still reeked of my former boyfriend, a painter named Arnold Janofsky who had left me over a year ago around the time my father died. The conjunction of the two events had leveled me for a while.

The novel was supposed to make up for everything that had gone wrong—I'd actually almost believed it would, but of course it didn't. In fact, as most first novelists discover, few people were aware my book had even come out. I was no less alone in the world than I'd been before, despite the different men I'd sometimes mistakenly bring home for company. I'd wake up daily in what my friend Elise Cowen once called in a poem "the black park of bed." Elise was the closest friend I'd ever had. A month after my novel was published, she'd jumped to her death from her parents' living-room window.

I was seriously thinking about Rome as a plausible destination. According to a girl I often talked with in the Cedar Bar, rooms were cheaper there than in Paris, and you could easily find work as an extra in Italian films. But the capital of everything I cared about was still a few square blocks of downtown New York.

When I was just twenty-one, in the summer of 1957, I'd walked into the Cedar Bar for the first time and discovered exactly the world I'd been looking for, a warm little republic of artists and writers, photographers, dancers, jazz musicians—many of them young and just as obscure as I was. But even the suddenly famous painters like Willem de Kooning and Franz Kline seemed remarkably open, unaccustomed to their recent success, their own long struggles very fresh in their memories. I'd still been with Kerouac when *On the Road* was published later that year, but even after we broke up, I considered myself extremely lucky to be living so much at the center of things—the full flowering of Beat writing and abstract expressionist painting—a remarkable period that had lasted five years and was now coming to an end, although I didn't realize it.

Back then all I knew was that the atmosphere had changed. Kerouac's notoriety had broken him. Painters were talking about tax deductions and the renovation of country houses; writers who had published each others' work in little magazines were becoming embittered and jealous. And the Cedar had been invaded by rich people, the kind Hemingway called "pilot fish," piling out of taxis on the weekends, pushing their way into the crowds three deep at the bar; artists were being courted by fashion models, who showed up in the most extraordinary outfits, or by young socialites back from Paris, like the woman my former boyfriend had left me for—tempted, I was certain, by the obvious advantages of her East Hampton connections. The old defiant innocence—the kind Jim brought with him when he arrived on the scene—was already no longer relevant.

When I was a junior at Barnard, I'd read a story by Nathaniel Hawthorne about a man named Wakefield who goes missing. Wakefield tells his wife he's going on a short journey; instead he moves into a room around the corner, changes his appearance, and leads a kind of half-life for the next twenty years, watching his "widowed" wife grow older with complete detachment until one day he walks back in, desiring the simple comfort of a warm hearth. Hawthorne had been inspired by a newspaper account of a similar case. What had troubled him deeply, while exciting his interest, was the lack of any real motivation to account for what the man had done. Wakefield's behavior was arbitrary, gratuitous—or existential, as I saw it. And that, I remember, is what made the story so compelling for me—that someone could decide on a dime to walk out on a safe, predictable existence. I was eighteen—very close to making my own flight from home. But Hawthorne's moral made so little impression upon me that I forgot it completely. It seemed there were penalties for life-changing disjunctures. "Amid the seeming confusion of our mysterious world," Hawthorne wrote, "individuals are so nicely adjusted to a system and systems to one another and to a whole, that, by stepping aside for a moment a man exposes himself to a fearful risk of losing his place altogether."

Jim had been married as long as Wakefield—ten years. He had

two little boys. He didn't expect he'd never see them again. The house in Painesville was filled with his art—from his first watercolors to a new series of red, white, and black canvases he believed were his most important works so far. The paint was still drying when he left. He walked out on a reputation he no longer cared about. He was—according to the *Painesville Telegraph*—Painesville's "widely known local artist."

I have some photos of Jim from his Painesville period; they were taken for the *Telegraph* about ten months before he entered my life. Wearing a garage mechanic's outfit encrusted with the spatterings that have flown off his brush, he turns from one of his canvases to face the camera, utterly spent. Another shot shows him delivering a large painting to his gallery in Cleveland, striding down a wet pavement, oblivious to a woman with an umbrella looking on in surprise as the wall-size abstraction sails past her. Then there's the shot from his last one-man show in which Jim's first wife also appears. I used to stare at this one, unable to connect the man I knew with the tall midwestern matron smiling graciously at her acquaintances. It seemed to have been taken in a country where the customs were different, where the wife of an artist would wear an orchid corsage to her husband's opening—no wife of an abstract expressionist would do that in New York. Another strange thing about that shot was my difficulty in recognizing Jim. I had the same difficulty when I looked at the man with the bristling mustache and the heavy round owlish glasses in the other two photos. At the opening, though, the camera had caught something the mustache and horn-rims couldn't completely hide—the agonized grimace on his face.

By the time I met Jim, both the mustache and the glasses were gone. And he never explained why he'd needed them. He had a tender mouth and deep-set eyes that had seen too much. The eyes no longer matched. The bone around the outside of the right one had been smashed in a fight. But he was proud of the fact that he had twenty-twenty vision. You could read his face like a book, as the saying goes.

"Can I buy you a drink?" was the second question he asked me, five days after the party. He'd been standing just behind me at the bar, but I hadn't noticed, hadn't seen him walk into the Cedar. When I turned and saw who it was, I said yes. But immediately after that things got a little confusing, because a sporadic boyfriend of mine—a married poet who was careful not to be seen with me too often—stepped away from a group of his friends and in a discreetly lowered voice made me the same offer. "No, thanks," I remember saying. "A gentleman is already getting me one." And that was how my relationship with the poet ended, then and there with no hard feelings on either side. But once he made Jim angry by telling him he thought I had a great smile. "What did he mean by *smile*?" Jim asked me.

I remember the weight with which Jim first told me his name. It was hardly an uncommon one, yet it seemed important to him that I understand how he came by it. His father, James Johnson, he said, was half Norwegian; the other half was Irish.

He'd been away from New York for ten years. I thought he was joking when he told me where he'd been living.

"I've been in Painesville."

"We've *all* been in Painesville," I said, but it turned out it was a real place. He said he'd come back to breathe—for days he'd been walking his feet off.

"I saw you," I told him, "the other day on Second Avenue."

"Why didn't you say hello?"

"I didn't know you."

"But you *remembered* me."

I'd been halfway in love with him since he'd asked me that question at the party. Because I did hang back. But even after we finally started talking, I was trying so hard to protect myself that everything I said to him at first seemed to go sideways. I remember he wanted to know if I came to the Cedar all the time. "Only in certain periods," I lied. I was very susceptible to a certain kind of man— maybe Kerouac had been the prototype—a man who didn't have caution in him, who said what he thought without filters. I never fell in love with anyone who needed to ask me what I was thinking.

"I'm going to Rome next month," I told Jim, because I thought he'd better know that immediately.

"So you're leaving, and I'm staying."

"That's New York for you."

"How about getting out of here?" he said.

He came from Lake Erie in the first novel I tried to write about him. Lake Erie had no symbolic overtones and it was in the same

part of Ohio, and he'd actually taught art at the women's college
there, the so-called "Vassar of the Midwest." Painesville, like his
real name, was a pitfall—an example of real life handing you
something so made-to-order for the purposes of fiction, it was
likely to make your readers roll their eyes. The story seemed full of
potential pitfalls of that sort. I called the Jim character Tom Jackson, but the name fell short—never conjured him.

I was thirty-five, seven years had passed, I had just walked out
on my second husband. I sat at the typewriter during the long
nights after I'd put my child to bed. The novel was supposed to
get me over things. I was going to use up the story by writing it—
neutralize it by giving it form. "After great pain," Emily Dicken-
son had written, "a formal feeling comes." I called the novel *A
Temporary Life.*

By the time I finished the second novel about Jim, fifteen years
later, I'd almost forgotten he had come from Painesville—I realized that with a start only recently.

The fiction keeps getting in the way, as if I'm remembering what I
wrote rather than what happened. But the walk in the first chapter
of the novel I gave up on is the one we actually took—all the way
down to Chinatown. And we did stop on our way back at the little
bar on Houston Street only Jim ever seemed to know about—the
mafia place with the great jukebox, where he told me he'd never
known his father.

I'd led into this revelation with the Jai Jai & Kai record playing
on the jukebox (providing a clue, consciously or not, to Tom Jackson's real identity, since Jai Jai was the jazz trombonist James Johnson). "The first thing I ever wanted to be," Tom Jackson says, "was
a musician. My old man played the trombone. Or so they told
me." The throwaway line I either gave him or remembered is very

loaded. All he can really tell the girl he's drinking with is that his father "split very early."

"Split very early" also rings a bell, though I'm no longer sure how the subject came up. Maybe Jim had been talking about his sons—how they'd grow up in a house with a big yard where they'd always have everything they needed and their lives would be peaceful now that he was gone. The name of the older one, the six-year-old, was Jimmy. Maybe I said something like, "Oh, another James Johnson," just to lighten things up a little.

I doubt the jukebox in that bar, which I think was called the Short Stop, played anything as esoteric as a recording by Jai Jai and Kai. It was the kind of place that had candles stuck in Chianti bottles and sawdust on the floor; we were sitting on barrels at a small round table. I remember staring at the ring Jim wore—silver with a dull red stone—and the crucial moment his hand took over mine. I remember the way he'd toss down a beer, then pass the back of his wrist over his mouth very quickly—the gesture that always killed me because it made him look like a kid. I remember him saying that when he told his wife he was leaving, she seemed utterly indifferent. Which I chose to believe.

The bar closed, and he said, "I'll walk you home." We were still both pretending we weren't necessarily going to bed with each other. In a few days he was supposed to call me to see if I'd heard of a studio for him. He needed a cheap loft right away so that he could briefly return to Ohio and bring all his paintings back in a truck. I'd written my phone number inside a matchbook. "Don't lose it now," I said, taking a chance on blowing my cool as I gave it to him.

He put it away carefully in his wallet. "I never lose anything important."

It was so late outside, the sky was beginning to get white. It was the hour when it's coldest and the streets are empty. Once walking home by myself in the unforgiving light, I'd seen de Kooning stumbling along First Avenue. The way Jim had his arm around me, de Kooning had had his arm around a gray-faced wraith of a woman—they looked as if they'd slept together in a doorway. He turned and smiled at me beatifically as they passed. "Oh," he said, "we've had such a *beautiful* night."

"Come upstairs for a minute," I said to Jim, still talking sideways as we hesitated, unwilling to part, outside the door of my building.

I no longer recall what we said to each other one flight up or our hungry, inexorable progress to the mattress on the floorboards of the front room. My memory fades out demurely like an old-fashioned movie. But the next scene comes up bathed in yellow light. It's morning—the sun is up over the low rooftops of the East Village, over the flat rubble field across First Avenue where blocks of tenements have recently been torn down, over the dusty tree with hard red buds just outside my window. The sun is in the room as I wake up, Jim's breath upon my back, his hands around my breasts. I lie there in astonishment, careful not to move.

I still remember all the apartments I lived in during my twenties along with their various idiosyncrasies—the one where I had to wash dishes in the bathroom sink; the one with the airshaft window and the evil superintendent; the one where the ceiling collapsed as I was making love with the married poet—the crevasse had been neatly replastered by the night I walked in with Jim.

I had little during that period in the way of worldly goods, but I'd accumulated some things I wanted to keep: an old round oak table I'd bought for twelve dollars, a rocking chair, a Peruvian rug Uncle Uda had brought up from South America, the Royal portable Aunt Anna had given me for my thirteenth birthday, two expensive red pots from France (for Arnold Janofsky I'd tried to master French cuisine in a week so that we could entertain the famous art dealer Leo Castelli). I also had a couple of hundred books, including a signed edition of *On the Road*—"From Amigo Jack," it said— and Elise's old copy of Apollinaire's poems. Whenever I thought about going to Rome, I worried about what would happen to all these belongings, not that they could possibly keep me in New York. But I was no Wakefield. Already I knew how memories settled on stuff like dust and that somewhere in that dust I made my home.

When I first moved into the apartment with the unreliable ceiling, I thought my life had taken an unexpected turn toward the bourgeois because the bathroom had tiles and because Arnold Janofsky took up all the layers of linoleum and scraped the floor and put a shelf up in the kitchen. Soon after we met, he had moved me into his studio on Second Avenue, then suddenly he'd decided he could no longer live right on top of his work—or maybe he was looking toward the near future when a new girl might catch his fancy and a place in which to leave me would be required.

I'd learned things from Arnold, not all of them bitter. He taught me how to make couscous and Moroccan chopped salad and how to arrange household objects in the manner of Cézanne or Matisse—here a green Chinese ginger jar, there a brown bowl of apples—so that they constituted potential still lifes. But when I came home triumphantly with the red pots, he'd derided me, the way I imagined a husband would, for spending too much money, even though every dollar I'd spent was mine. Up till then, my heart had been set on marrying him, but the kind of marriage I'd envisioned did not include fights about red pots. Maybe marriage, in its usual sense, was never what I wanted. Maybe I was looking for a love affair that would never end.

With Jim there never would be time enough for entropy to set in. "We can't slow this down," he said the first of the six hundred mornings we woke up together, the morning I opened my eyes and thought *Found* in the apartment where I'd been so unhappy. It looked beautiful to me again in the light pouring in through the unwashed windows.

"I like this place," Jim said to me as we were having coffee. "I like it because you've left it bare. There should never be too much in a room."

"Maybe you could take it over after I leave," I said, my heart beating faster because I couldn't let go of my disbelief and felt I had to test him. "You could look after my stuff while I'm gone."

He looked at me across the round table and called my bluff. "But I'm going to marry you. I can't do it yet, but it will happen."

It was about a week before he officially moved in, though we spent every minute we could together. He'd been staying farther downtown with Ron Gorchov, whom he'd known since art school. Gorchov seemed amazed that Jim had made his mind up about a woman so quickly.

He'd arrived in New York almost empty-handed, but he too had stuff—it followed him from Painesville by Greyhound, traveling more slowly and circuitously than he had. I accompanied him to the freight office the day he went to claim it and bring it to the apartment. Leaving the bright streets, together we walked through the bus terminal, hand in hand. Pimps and whores from Eighth Avenue were transacting their business; old people and winos who had come out of the cold dozed on long plastic benches; an exhausted mother screamed at her three small children. "Poor people's transportation," Jim said.

He had four yellow tickets, which he presented to a clerk behind a counter. The man disappeared and came back with three items: a gray suitcase, the box in which Jim had packed his trombone, a heavy roll of canvas wrapped in torn brown paper.

Jim said another suitcase was missing that had been shipped at the same time. But the clerk wasn't interested. It got separated, the clerk said, it maybe got put in Unclaimed. As their voices rose, the people waiting behind us started shifting from one foot to another, trying to get a look.

The clerk wanted Jim to fill out a form—no one had time to look for a suitcase with no number. "Then the form isn't worth shit!" Jim said in a loud, terrible voice that made everyone freeze. I remember putting my hand on his arm, but he didn't seem to notice. By now there was a boy standing beside the clerk with a fixed, expectant smile.

I came from people who never raised their voices—even the most awful things were said quietly. If I had been Jim, I'd have filled out the form and gone home. Yet the part of me praying he would do that filled me with shame.

What he did next—in one rash move—made dumbfounding sense. With one hand braced on the countertop, he vaulted over to the other side. "Where's Unclaimed?" he demanded as the clerk backed away.

"What do you want to know that for?"

"Because I'm going there—that's why."

The clerk took out a handkerchief and rubbed his forehead with it. He told the boy to get the supervisor, but the boy, still grinning, said the supervisor was out to lunch. The clerk rubbed his forehead some more, then the back of his neck. "Okay," he said finally. "Take him to Unclaimed. But you stay with him."

"My friend's coming with us," Jim said.

Unclaimed was lit very dimly. Rows of metal racks rose to the ceiling, crowded with bulging cartons, shopping bags stuffed with clothes, lost guitars, bicycles, overcoats, portable radios, innumerable brown suitcases like the one Jim was trying to find. Every unclaimable thing there must have been important to someone. "Go ahead—take a look," the boy said with a shrug.

I trailed after Jim as he silently started down a row, pulling things aside, shoving them back. I knew he would search every shelf in the place if he had to. After a while I stopped following him. I kept thinking we were at the bottom of the world.

He'd started down another row when he stopped in his tracks. "Got it!" he cried out in triumph.

On our way downtown in a taxi, he noticed I wasn't saying much. "That guy wasn't about to fight me. Don't you think I knew?"

I looked out the window feeling shame again and said I wasn't sure.

He laughed. "You're right. I would have pushed it all the way."

He opened the suitcases on the bed in the apartment. Out of the gray one, he pulled a dark suit and a couple of neckties—"Something tells me I'm not going to be wearing these much"—then a striped sailor's jersey he said he'd bought the year he and his wife had lived in Paris: "It's yours if you want it." It's true I never wore it much, but I held on to it for years. Jim liked to give me things, and for me that was a new experience—it was the first of all his gifts.

The suitcase he had fought for was full of what my mother might have called "things of value." There were tubes of paint—the cadmium red was very expensive, he told me; brushes wrapped in aluminum foil; a staple gun; an electric saw; a knife that seemed particularly important to him—he showed me how neatly the blade folded into its black handle. He used that knife, he said, for just about everything—fishing, slitting canvas, carving roasts, you name it; I remember him showing me the place where his thumb had worn away the finish on the wood. He'd been troubled by the thought that in his rush he'd forgotten to pack his knife.

A small metal box contained a collection of papers and identification cards: in 1950, he'd been a member in good standing of the Art Students League; in 1946 he'd signed up for the Merchant Marine, and they'd taken a tiny snapshot of a boy with unruly hair and riveting melancholy eyes. There were ribbons and overseas medals

in that box, a document stating that the U.S. Navy would take care
of his burial, to which he called my attention for some reason I was
reluctant to understand, and a black photostat of his birth certificate. He unfolded it so that I could see his father's signature. There
it was in ghostly white: James Johnson, age 20, cabdriver. His address seemed ghostly, too—34 Old Broadway; I'd never heard of
an Old Broadway in New York City.

I felt as if Jim were unpacking *himself*—the portable compo-
nents of who he was—before my eyes, as if he needed someone to
corroborate that the James Johnson Jr. whose name kept appearing
so persistently really existed.

A green scrapbook at the bottom of the suitcase was half filled
with clippings and photos from his former life. I kept turning the
pages hoping to see pictures of his two little boys. Already I'd was
trying to imagine the child he and I would have someday—I was
twenty-six; it was time. But all the stuff in the scrapbook had to do
with his career. I wondered if he had any snapshots of the kids in
his wallet. One day he told me he'd thrown them away in the
men's room of the bus terminal in Cleveland. So that he wouldn't
be tempted to go right back to them. So that he wouldn't be reminded of what he'd done.

The morning after we brought the suitcases home, I woke up
thinking I heard rain, but it was a shower of cadmium red thud-
ding against the canvas Jim had stapled to the wall opposite the
bed. He'd gotten up hours ago, pulled up the blinds so he
wouldn't have to turn on a light; already a painting was materializ-
ing. Ever since he moved in, he'd been staring hungrily at that
wall, thinking there'd just be room enough for three paintings, but
he'd warned me that he tended to work large. How large? I'd asked
him, and he'd grinned and said I'd see. When he'd unrolled his

canvas the night before, he'd cut off the piece that now stretched from the floor to the ceiling.

Arnold had never let me put anything on that wall; he had contempt for people who put up prints, but he'd never brought any of his own paintings over. When we lived in his studio, he'd shut the door behind him when he went into his work area and would only invite me to come in when he thought he'd finished something. But Jim didn't seem to mind that I was right there. "Stay in bed, kiddo," he told me. "You want to see this, don't you? This painting's for you anyway."

It was like watching a dance. I'd never fully realized how *physical* painting could be. It wasn't like writing a story, creeping along a blank page the way I did one word at a time. There was something so immediate about the way he worked, the visible connection between his eye and his hand. With only a few of his broad strokes different paintings kept coming into being, each one blooming for a while with exploding constellations of reds and pinks, blacks and grays, before a series of other rapid strokes would obliterate it. He seemed to be painting speed onto the canvas. How would he know when he was finished? I wondered as I watched him lost in his dance, bending to the cans of paint on the floor, charging forward with his brush, stepping back, bending again. Was there a vision of how it was supposed to look in his mind? Or did he leave that to be discovered?

"A painting isn't finished," he said once, "until you sign your name to it."

The apartment was small; its two rooms opened into each other railroad-style. We slept in the one with windows. When the wall was filled, there was no space to do another painting until the first ones dried and could be rolled up, but there was no good place to put the roll. We started asking everyone we knew whether they'd heard of a loft we could move into. "Look downtown," people said, "there's nothing in the Village or around Tenth Street these days." The success of the abstract expressionists had caused a gold rush of hopeful artists to descend upon New York. The owners of abandoned factory buildings below Fourteenth Street were having a field day.

We bought the paper every day, but nothing we could afford was advertised. Every time we went anywhere, we'd look up at loft windows, hoping to spot the For Rent sign that would change our luck. Our best hope was the Bowery, where buildings were unheated and bums slept in the doorways. A few artists were even living in Chinatown. When Jim finally heard about a place on Chrystie Street from a painter he'd met at the Cedar, he rushed right down there while I was at work and decided immediately that we'd take it. It was twenty-five hundred square feet—room enough to last him the rest of his life, he said.

A sculptor had been living there who'd put in a bathroom and a kitchen. The guy was a weird character, according to Jim. He'd given up sculpture and was building a twenty-foot catamaran right in the loft, which he planned to move out through the front windows and sail to the Bahamas. He needed five hundred dollars from us to finish his work on the wooden pontoons before hurricane season; then he'd be gone, and we could take the place over. The pontoons, Jim said, were amazing—pure forms like Brancusi's—a hundred times better than the sculptor's other work.

I still had the five hundred dollars that had been supposed to take me to Rome. I felt very lucky to have the money for the sculptor's pontoons, for the coats of sealer or whatever it was that he needed.

Chrystie Street runs downtown behind the Bowery from Houston Street all the way to the stone foundations of the Manhattan

Bridge, where it ends abruptly, although the Bowery continues on past Canal Street. Our loft building was in the middle of the block between Grand and Hester. Last time I looked, it was still there, renovated and divided into apartments. And the forlorn strip of park we could see from our front windows is there, too, and only a little less forlorn. All the names on the buzzers are Chinese. That whole section of Chrystie Street is part of Chinatown now, a different neighborhood from the one I remember. In our day, our block was the last outpost of Little Italy; you'd cross the park and land on Forsyth Street in Puerto Rican territory.

We used to think of Grand Street as the Boulevard of Cut-rate Brides. The shopwindows were filled with ancient veiled mannequins in yellowing gowns and their garishly attired attendants. Bums would sleep at the feet of the brides in blue halos of fluorescent light. "We'll have to buy you one of those gowns," Jim would tease me. We were planning to be married by the fall, or as soon as Jim could get a divorce.

Our building stood between a tenement with a downstairs store occupied by a friendly butcher with mafia connections and an auto repair shop. On the ground floor was the office of our landlord, a plumber; on the second floor a fishing-fly factory had abruptly gone out of business years before—the owner had simply locked up one day and left. Our loft was just upstairs. Above us was a derelict space where pigeons had gotten in and made nests.

The sculptor told us the building had been condemned in 1927 because of some structural defect. But, hey, it was still standing. "So much for the experts!" the sculptor said, adding that a housing inspector might bother us but could probably be paid off. Certainly the seventy-five-dollar rent made a little uncertainty worthwhile.

He'd grown tired of trying to be an artist in New York. Better to live on fish and rice somewhere closer to the equator on the wooden platform he was going to attach to his two pontoons. The sculptor had previously worked in stone. He left us a chunk of black granite that we used as a coffee table. In the loft upstairs amid the calcified bird droppings and pigeon feathers were jagged segments of marble torsos that he'd smashed with a sledgehammer.

"These are the best times we'll ever have," I remember Jim saying that summer, soon after we'd moved in. I can't remember what prompted that statement, but I remember the way he said it, with absolute gravity and almost sadly. As I look back, there's the feeling of prophecy about it. "These are the best times we'll ever have."

Oddly enough, I think we'd just had a fight, because we did have fights at times even then, usually when he'd been drinking and saw his life in excruciating black-and-white terms. He'd utter something that must have seemed devastatingly profound, which he wouldn't recall by the following morning, and yell at me for not paying sufficient attention. Or he'd yell at me because I was frail in some way, because in his estimation I'd let myself down.

It bothered him that he seldom saw me working at my type-writer, or that I'd been with men before him who had treated me badly. Once he asked me about Arnold—why I'd put up with him for two years.

With embarrassment I said something like, "Because there was a gap in my life, and he filled it."

"And so I fill it now—real easy?"

Maybe I ended up in tears, and that's when he said that eerie thing that made everything all right again and turned out to be true.

I wasn't troubled at first about the drinking. Everyone drank in the small downtown world I knew, although I didn't care much for alcohol myself. In the Cedar Bar artists still pointed out with a certain pride the famous door through which Jackson Pollock had once been ejected, with the little round window in which his bloodshot eye had appeared as he pleaded to be let back in. There were legends about the outrageous things de Kooning had said to other painters when he was too far gone to stand up. "Get out of my aura!" I heard him thunder at a minor abstractionist who had sat down in his booth one night. The painters had a rough-and-tumble style—even the women painters were macho. Drink seemed to go with the territory. There was something about the riskiness of abstract expressionist painting, the sheer hubris of the desire to put something on canvas no one had ever seen before, the terror of failing or running dry, that led to the need to keep seeking oblivion. Or maybe there were lives like Jim's that resulted in certain kinds of artists.

He was actually trying *not* to drink when I met him—or at least not to drink too much. It was very soon after that spin on the ice. There seemed to be a lot of gray Volvos in New York like the one he'd had in Painesville. As we walked along together, he'd stop a moment if he saw one parked—"That was *my* car—same model, same color, fantastic brakes. They know how to make cars in Sweden." He was sure he'd be dead several times over if it hadn't been for the Volvo. He'd get one again if he ever had the chance, or the money.

But at present money was what he didn't have. It would only start coming in again when he was able to bring his paintings to New York and find himself a gallery. He had always been able to sell some of his work, even some of the watercolors he'd done at the Art Students League when he was studying with John Marin and Reginald Marsh. He told me how he used to amuse himself painting perfect mirror images, working with both his left hand and his right. He'd show me those little watercolors when his work arrived from Painesville. Meanwhile he was burning with ideas and couldn't even afford to buy canvas. As we waited for the sculptor to move out, he took a job, temporarily, at a market research firm— something to do with transferring data to coded cards.

I was used to offices—Jim had never worked in one. I'd had secretarial jobs in publishing ever since I'd been on my own, and lately, at William Morrow, I'd been promoted to copyeditor. But I was becoming more ambitious—I'd shown a brilliant book about jazz by a friend of mine, the poet LeRoi Jones, to the editor-in-chief, and talked him into publishing it. I knew the right lingo— you didn't want to sound too passionate: this unknown black writer was the wave of the future, I said, and here was a chance for our company to get in on the ground floor. On weekday mornings I'd slip into my uptown personality along with nylons and shirt-waist dresses, suppressing any urges to stay home and write. At lunches with virginal office friends, who were mostly working for pin money and a little worldly experience, I'd stop short of revealing I was living with a man. It reminded me of acting, and I'd always been able to act.

But because Jim had left so much identity behind in Painesville, he always carried with him everything that remained. During his first week as a market researcher, he'd hurry to fill in his quotas of cards, then secretly do pencil drawings to run through the Thermofax machine, trying to convince himself he was fascinated by the way the greasy, yellowish copy paper would alter the texture. I remember how depressed he was when he got his paycheck. It wasn't even a hundred dollars, when just a few months before a Cleveland collector had come to his studio and bought the very painting he'd started that morning for eight hundred bucks. "Not bad," he said, "for a day's work."

He started going out to lunch with his fellow freelance employees, out-of-work actors and others down on their luck—a few drinks with these men would make the afternoon go faster, and by the time I met him at the Cedar after work he'd already be a little lit, a little more intense. Once we went from the Cedar to the gallery opening of an artist he knew. The artist was an amiable guy, but his paintings were weak, and Jim couldn't restrain himself from muttering to me, "Which one of these do you want me to put my foot through?" "Derivative shit," he said in a voice loud enough to make people turn and stare. I remember having to beg him to leave and Jim being angry with me until he woke up sober and contrite the next morning. He didn't arrive at work until eleven that day and walked out when his supervisor said, "What's the matter, Johnson? Been up all night with a sick painting?"

When he hit the street, Jim headed for the Cedar. There he ran into de Kooning, the only other customer at the bar. "I'm a Leo," de Kooning boasted. "I'm a Leo," Jim said.

De Kooning had shown Jim his left hand. "I have this line that runs straight across—the meeting of heart and mind. No one else has this line."

That night Jim told me that when he'd glanced at his own hand, he'd found the de Kooning line there, too.

Office work was too confining for him, he'd decided. He'd be better off supporting himself by doing carpentry and house painting. He spent part of his last paycheck on a silver bracelet for me. When he ran out of money later that month, he hocked his trombone.

A few weeks after we moved into the loft, the lawyer we hoped would handle Jim's divorce came down to Chrystie Street for brunch and to see which paintings were available. He was a fortyish man with a smooth bedside manner who liked to think of himself as a collector and hang out with his artist clients. I think it was the sculptor who recommended him. If someone's work fitted in with his decor, this lawyer would take a painting in lieu of a fee.

He arrived an hour late with a woman in big dark glasses and a rumpled yellow dress she must have have wearing the night before, wherever he'd found her. Whenever she swiveled around in her seat and crossed her legs to lean toward Jim, her short skirt would ride up on her skinny thighs and the yellow silk would fall away from her breasts in a manner that did not seem accidental. "Bagel or toast?" I asked her loudly at one point. She tore her eyes away from Jim for a moment and coldly sized me up. "How long have you two been together?" she inquired.

The lawyer seemed unperturbed that this woman was paying no attention to him. He had recently purchased an orange couch, and that couch seemed very much on his mind whenever he got up from the table to pace in front of the three paintings Jim had done in the apartment. After several trips into the studio, he wanted to know whether I'd be open to negotiation for the one Jim told him he had given to me. I didn't know what to answer, but Jim cut in and said, "No deal, Elliott. You can have either of the other two, or come back another time," as if he'd forgotten how much depended upon getting this lawyer to work for him, since there was no way he could afford one otherwise.

The lawyer laughed and said Jim was a tough customer, and that there was certainly something "sort of powerful" about the paintings—it was about the fourth time he had used that particular adjective—which obviously "went along with the territory," as he put it. "But there's red in all of them. I don't know about the red."

"You could always get rid of the couch, Elliott," Jim said. I could tell he was concentrating on being patient, but something flashed in his voice that reminded me of that moment in the bus station just before he'd leapt over the counter.

Fortunately the lawyer assumed Jim couldn't be serious. The orange couch, he calmly explained, had been custom-made for him in Italy by a famous designer—by which I knew he meant you did not get rid of such a couch because of a canvas by an artist without a name. But right after that, he said the painting that had the least red was starting to grow on him, and then it was agreed that Jim would bring it up to his apartment so that it could be tried out and the lawyer measured it carefully with a tape measure he had brought. As if it were being sold by the yard, I thought indignantly, though I was relieved that once the dangerous moments had passed, things had turned out well.

After the lawyer had gone, Jim looked at me and said, "I've always sold my work to fools."

About Jim's wife, I knew little. I remember having an image of her at first as a tiny dark figure at the vanishing point of tracks going back into Jim's past—as if years instead of weeks had gone by since that night in Painesville when he'd told her he was leaving. During the final months of their marriage, his wife had become obsessed with doing crossword puzzles, he told me. The ones in the daily paper weren't enough for her—she'd buy herself books of crosswords and sit up into the small hours with her sharpened pencils and her thesaurus and a bowl of potato chips, and he'd hear her teeth coming down on each chip with a snap as she worked, completely shutting him out. He'd come home the night he'd almost wrecked the Volvo, and there she was at the kitchen table as usual—snap, snap—barely looking up as he walked in.

I wonder sometimes whether he would have stayed if she'd looked at him that night with pain or love or even rage, but whatever she felt, she evidently preferred to conceal. He was the kind of man who couldn't help churning up the air. He said his wife once told him there was nothing she wanted more than silence in her house. Well, he gave her that all right, he supposed, when he left. He imagined she would remarry quickly, find herself someone totally unlike him—maybe a professor from the college where she taught, some quiet, tweedy, pipe-smoking Anglophile who'd take her for vacations in the Lake District and get the stamp of approval from her family.

Jim was bitter about his wife's family. They were powerful people in Cleveland, high society. They could trace their roots to British colonists in Virginia, while he could only trace his to a tenement in Hell's Kitchen. I remember he'd never eat strawberries because his father-in-law was especially fond of them—there were always strawberries at the in-laws' luncheons where Jim had to put in an appearance—strawberries and whipped cream—and he'd sit with the third stiff drink he'd ordered in front of him, watching his father-in-law wipe the pink cream off his lips with a linen napkin. Something the old man had said to him early on—that maybe the bloodlines would be enriched now that Jim was marrying into the family—should have let him know where he stood.

Jim's in-laws had been the hosts of a curious gathering on the evening of May 20, 1951, a buffet dinner and art exhibition to mark the engagement of their daughter. "With tongue in cheek and a twinkle in the eye," reported a society columnist for the *Cleveland Plain Dealer,* "they put one over" on their guests, "for the invitations were inscribed in part 'To Meet the Artist,'" though the artist himself was a thousand miles away in Manhattan in his fiancée's apartment, where a simultaneous party with an identical menu was going on, connected to the festivities in the Midwest by a long-distance phone call. The absent artist was represented at the Cleveland party by a display of his watercolors, several of which had won prizes.

Among the invited guests at the party in Manhattan was "Mrs. James Whearty of New York," the woman Jim never wanted me to meet. It's weird to see that name in a society column, but there it is in print—Mrs. Whearty's only claim to fame. After that evening she would not see much of the son she had given birth to at seventeen, the unwanted child with the maddening resemblance to his father—"You look like him, you act like him," she had said to Jim accusingly all through his boyhood. He'd been told that his mother had been in the habit of putting him in his baby carriage and leaving him out on the street unattended for a good part of the day; once a crazy woman who happened to be passing by had heard the infant crying inconsolably and attempted to kidnap him but had been stopped by a neighbor in the nick of time. He could remember his mother taking him into speakeasies when he was very little, putting him to bed on a couple of chairs in a corner and once under a pool table while she made out with some guy on top.

She had never warmed toward him, even after she became Mrs. Whearty. Her second husband was a hard-drinking British seaman who had jumped ship in New York; by him she had another son she liked a little better than the first one. When Jim was seventeen and lied about his age to join the navy, she was only too glad to sign the papers that would make her the beneficiary of compensation in the event of his death.

I picture a rouged and graying "Mrs. James Whearty of New York" among the high-spirited art students and the well-bred graduates of Ivy League colleges at the engagement party. "Don't mind if I do," she says with a shrill laugh whenever someone offers to refill her glass. In my mind, she has always emitted a dangerous radioactive glitter. Theoretically, she could still be alive—a hundred years old. I inherited her with the rest of Jim's history. It could be said she darkened my life, too.

* * *

Jim's half brother, Bob Whearty, lived up in the Bronx, somewhere near Fordham Road, as I remember. He was a cop, and he looked older than Jim, though he was five years younger, a burly man with a soft Irish face and sad pale blue eyes. He had a sweet wife and two small children—he was very tender with his kids. We went up there for dinner. The Wheartys were shy with me, elaborately polite, insistent on second helpings. There was a painting of Jim's in their living room. "I still don't know what to make of it, but I like it," Bob Whearty said.

At one point he looked across the table at Jim and said, "Well, are you going to go and see them?" and I knew he was talking about their mother and Jim's stepfather. "Don't tell them I'm back," Jim answered. "Don't tell them I'm getting divorced. They don't have to know anything about me."

Bob Whearty said he saw them, not too often, maybe every month or so. Sometimes he brought food over because the old man was sick with diabetes, wasn't doing too well.

But Jim didn't want the details. "It's different for you, Bobby."

I saw Bob Whearty's eyes grow even sadder. "Yeah," he said. "You were the one who always got beat up on. How do you think that made me feel?"

A letter Jim's father-in-law wrote him in 1952 is pasted into his scrapbook among the clippings about Midwest art shows and prizes—preserved like a certificate of the acceptance Jim must have hoped for at first.

"Dear Jimmy my boy: (Irish to the end!)" the letter begins, the effusive tone disguising what I suspect was the ambivalence of the writer. The father-in-law had just gone to see a watercolor of Jim's entitled *Urbana* that was being shown in Cleveland with works by several hundred other artists and thought Jim would like to have the photo he had taken there. But he also made a point of enclosing a photo of the watercolor seascape hanging right alongside *Urbana.* That particular artist, he noted, was "an old rich Cleveland industrialist" who only painted during his summer vacations on Cape Cod.

*Urbana* was an industrial river scene, all roiling blacks and grays, shot through with light, just on the edge of abstraction. Jim's father-in-law had been asked by two or three of his friends whether it depicted a sunrise, to which he had cannily replied that it would be "safer to call it a landscape mood." Right after that, he added: "Proud of you."

"Affectionately thine," he signed off. Then came what I imagine was the most powerful word for his son-in-law in the whole letter:

"Dad."

Trouble arrived in the mail one day in July in a cream-colored envelope from Painesville. The wife who had longed so much for quiet did not seem to be as indifferent to Jim's departure as he had imagined. Although she had done nothing to persuade Jim to stay with her, she claimed she had been "abandoned," according to the brief her lawyer was ready to present in court. Yet she was demanding neither child support nor alimony. What she seemed to want instead was retribution, mistakenly believing that would alleviate her pain. She would never allow Jim to see his sons again—in fact, he was to be prohibited from even setting foot in the state of Ohio. As for the paintings he had left behind, she would never release any of them to him—not one watercolor—under any circumstances. They would gather dust in Painesville, where the art world would never get to look at them. He would have to start all over again—from nothing—if he had the heart for it.

She seemed to know him inside out, the husband who had left her, with his anguished attachment to his kids, with his big dreams of having his paintings hung in museums, with his terrible childhood, his demons, his tenderness, his hubris—everything she must have loved him for once and perhaps still did. But her wounds were very fresh.

After Jim read the letter, he told me for the first time something she had said to him the night he told her he was going to New York: "You're doing to your kids what your father did to you."

The paintings and the kids—those huge lost pieces of himself— were always on Jim's mind after that, even when he didn't seem to be thinking about them. The lawyer told him there was little he could do in view of the charge of abandonment—and after all, he pointed out, Jim was lucky his wife wasn't asking for money. The lawyer came down to the loft for a second visit and selected another, larger painting—this one for his office—which would cover the additional expenses of the proceedings.

"I can always paint more," Jim would say. "Of course you will," I'd tell him. He'd go into the studio and pick up his brushes again, but he'd find no joy or certainty in the work, and he'd tear the canvas off the wall, the staples popping out of the plaster, then walk into the back room and pull a beer out of the refrigerator. "I have a terrible thirst," he'd say to me.

Sometimes I thought I could almost understand what Jim's wife had done—I could recognize the impulse. When Arnold had moved back into his loft with his new girlfriend from East Hampton, he forgot to pack his collection of jazz records, which he'd kept in the apartment. He'd had many of those LPs for years— they meant something to him. I refused to let him come by to pick them up. "There's nothing you can take out of here, Arnold," I'd told him. But now he could have had them if he'd asked me. I wondered whether Jim's wife would ever reach that point of indifference. But then I'd never cared for Arnold as much I cared for Jim, and a record collection could be replaced.

One night Jim made a long-distance call to Painesville. In a voice that terrified me, he screamed at his wife until she hung up on him. I begged him not to call her again—it would only make things worse. He said he was thinking about renting a truck, driving it to Ohio, grabbing the kids as well as the paintings. I asked him if he was serious about this, and he said he thought about it every day. "You'd end up in jail," I told him. "What do I care?" he answered. I asked him, Didn't he care about me, about us? By then I was crying, and he was crying too. We held on to each other and wept until finally he managed to say something funny and I laughed, and he said, "You don't know whether you're laughing or crying."

But the impulse to rent the truck stayed with him—it must have been the only idea he could come up with about how to make himself whole. It was the way he had always resolved things—directly, physically—no more implausible to him than that leap in the bus terminal.

I was at the office the day Jim phoned U-Haul and found out the price of a rental. He'd just been paid for a carpentry job, so he had enough money in his pocket. He left the loft and headed uptown for the vehicle, figuring he'd call me later from somewhere on the road.

When I came home that night, however, he was waiting for me with a present—a thin gold ring with tiny emerald chips and moonstones that he'd found in a pawnshop. "You've got the truck on your finger now, kiddo," he said. "I blew all my money on it."

Lying in bed some mornings, eyes closed, I revisit the loft on Chrystie Street, drifting through the downstairs hallway, then up the two steep flights of steps that smell of dust and old dry wood. I unlock the door to which I long ago lost the key, and pass through the studio with the two big front windows where around six o'clock Jim would often stand smoking, looking down the street for me, with one foot on the sill. The coffee cans I used to save for him are still lined up on the worktable, filled with paint; the phonograph is playing Ray Charles or Dinah Washington; the cigarettes of the day are stubbed out in the hollow of a stone the sculptor left. On a wall are the latest canvases, utterly blank because I can no longer see what is on them, though if I try very hard, cloudlike shadows appear.

In the room in back it's always morning. I see my round oak table and the kitchen counter Jim built for me in one day out of plywood he found on the street. The gray cat is asleep in the brightest circle of sunlight from the alley; the new leaves of the avocado tree suspended in the mayonnaise jar are aglow. I'm up in the high bed the sculptor built above the clothes closet, lying next to Jim under the red blanket; any minute he will reach for me and whisper, "Scrooch over." I remember thinking, I don't need anything more than this. Even after things got very bad, there were still times when I'd have that thought.

We went uptown to see my mother and tell her we'd be getting married. Jim put on his suit for the occasion. It was the first time the two of them were going to meet, though I'd been dropping his name into our phone conversations so that she'd get used to the idea of this new "boyfriend." It had been years since she'd known very much about how I was actually living. She'd listen to what I chose to tell her and ask very few questions as an odd tight smile appeared on her face—a tea-party smile—the kind she might give to a mere acquaintance. Even when we were on the phone I could sometimes feel that smile forming.

I'd brought Arnold uptown too—several times while my father was still alive. Apart from the fact that we were living in sin, I didn't have to lie too much about Arnold Janofsky. He was Jewish, unencumbered by a previous wife, a moderate drinker with charming company manners. He even had a certain hardheadedness that must have been reassuring to my parents—I remember my father solemnly listening as Arnold explained that it was entirely possible for a successful painter to have an annual income equivalent to that of a doctor. All that was lacking was the announcement of a proposal of marriage. I used to wonder if my father died thinking my engagement to Arnold was probably just around the corner. "You're beautiful," he whispered the last time I saw him in the hospital, as if he forgave me for all the grief I'd ever caused him.

I felt my father's absence the night I introduced my mother to Jim. She was preparing the usual ceremonial dinner—leg of lamb with roasted potatoes and pressure-cooked string beans and carrots. She still cooked as if my father were alive, everything as plain and bland as it had been throughout my childhood due to his special diet. His death hadn't launched her into wild experiments with garlic and pepper or rearrangements of the furniture in the living room. My father could have been expected home any minute—as if the subway bringing him uptown from the office were just a little later than usual. If he had been there himself, he would have brought out the ancient bottle of scotch reserved for the visits of my uncles and poured a little into a glass for Jim. Instead it was my mother who went to locate the bottle. When she offered Jim a refill after he'd emptied his glass, he shook his head, with a quick glance at me. "No, I'm fine, Mrs. Glassman."

He hadn't been fine for weeks, really, but that night the clouds seemed to have lifted, and I watched my mother fall under his spell. She had started filling some of her time with art classes. I remember Jim with his head bent toward my mother, giving her his full attention as she chattered to him about her watercolor classes at the Y. "My teacher is Japanese," she said, as if this were a guarantee of the man's special gifts.

Jim said he'd been very much influenced by Japanese painting himself, the calligraphy especially. Someday soon he hoped she would come and see his work, though he only used oils and acrylics now. My mother grew pink-cheeked and girlish and said she'd love to.

I was the tongue-tied one at the table, distractedly waiting for the right opening in the conversation—the moment after the helpings of lamb, after the lettuce and tomato salad, the whipped raspberry Jell-O, when I would tell my mother the big true thing I was going to do with my life that she'd better not try to talk me out of. Meanwhile she was shyly offering Jim a tip, if he ever went back to doing watercolors—"You can hang them up to dry on the refrigerator with magnets. I know this sounds silly, but it works."

"I'll bear that in mind, Mrs. Glassman," Jim said gravely, and then suddenly both of them were smiling at each other.

"Mrs. Glassman," he said very soon after that, because I still hadn't geared myself up to give her our news, "Joyce and I actually came up here to tell you something. . . ."

My mother stared at the two of us and grew even pinker. "Oh," she said, her eyes filling, "I think I know what it is!"

My aunts were living in an apartment upstairs—they and my grandmother had moved into the building when I was fourteen. Now that my father was gone, there was little separation between the three sisters. They had keys to each other's apartments, so no one would be put to the trouble of getting stiffly up from a chair and going to the door—two quick rings, and they'd enter. My mother did the shopping for both establishments, keeping a sharp eye on the specials in the supermarket; on summer evenings, the three sisters would put on their hats after dinner and occupy a bench on Riverside Drive, watching the couples and dog walkers stroll by, breathing in the night air under the dusty elms no longer scented by my father's cigar. She phoned my aunts that night as soon as we'd finished dinner and excitedly told them to come down to meet "Joyce's new fiancé."

"It will be good to have another man in the family," Aunt Anna said after she and Jim had been introduced.

When we got home that night, he astonished me by announcing he'd decided to become Jewish so that we could have a Jewish wedding—"I don't want there to be any difference between us."

He told me that when he was a kid in the Bronx, Jewish housewives would call to him from their windows on Saturday afternoons asking him to come upstairs and light the stove; he'd kept hoping that one of them would offer to adopt him.

"You should be nicer to your mother," he said once. "If anything happened to me, you'd be alone just like her."

By the end of that summer, I'd stopped even attempting to write the novel I'd begun before I met Jim. When I sat at the typewriter, all I could do was shove words around idly like a child rearranging peas and carrots on a plate. It troubled Jim that I'd put my book aside, that I didn't even try to start something new. I should be like him, he'd tell me. Look how he picked himself up and went into the studio each day, although sometimes he hardly knew what he was doing in there—just that what he painted would end up either on the wall or on the floor. "If you're not going to write anymore," he'd challenge me fiercely, "just tell me you're going to forget about it. Go on—tell me you're going to forget the whole damn business."

I hated our conversations about why I wasn't writing. Sometimes I couldn't help thinking it was because everything was so uncertain, so difficult—our lack of money, his drinking, his divorce, the ex-boyfriends of mine he kept running into at the Cedar. Sometimes I thought it was our love that left no room, because I'd never known anything like it before. It was the real thing, equal on both sides. I knew it was the reason he sometimes drove me crazy by caring so much about what I did with my life.

Maybe I wasn't writing because the novel Jim and I were living had overwhelmed the one I was trying to make up, or because part of me had begun listening for something—something still far off but gradually, steadily gaining on us.

He'd begun talking about his kids and his father more and more as if there were no separation between the two subjects, as if he and his son Jimmy were almost the same person, as if all his memories were so entangled they formed one giant knot in his head. He thought the two-year-old, Bobby, would probably have little real memory of him; Jimmy, on the other hand, would be asking about him all the time, because he knew he'd been around just long enough to form him. He could imagine his son at sixteen running away from home to find him—turning up on Chrystie Street with a lot of questions.

I could tell he felt especially in touch with Jimmy whenever he took me fishing that summer. We didn't have a car, but on weekends we'd ride the subway out to Sheepshead Bay. Jim would buy clams, and we'd cut them up for bait out on a pier where neighborhood kids would watch him cast off. "Catch anything, mister?"

they'd ask. Occasionally he'd reel in a flounder or a blowfish or a horseshoe crab, but mostly the hours would melt away in a sunlit stillness. Jim would keep his eyes on the fixed point of the line in the water, and I'd sit beside him, trying to empty my mind of everything but the line's gentle fluctuations. We were always safe on that pier from the thing I'd started to listen for.

He'd often told me about fishing for stripers with Jimmy off a pier on Lake Erie, only a short drive from their house. The kid, Jim said, had incredible patience; he was only five years old, but he understood about keeping quiet. He'd even come into the studio while Jim was working and just sit in a corner, drawing pictures. As soon as Jimmy was big enough not to tumble into the water, he'd bought him his own fishing rod, and one afternoon the kid actually managed to catch a fish. Mish the Fish, Jimmy had called it. It was too small to eat, but they'd taken it home with them anyway, and Jim had dipped it in ink, which he said was a Japanese custom, and made a print of it for his son. "Now this fish can never be forgotten," he'd told him.

He thought he might have met his own father when he was around Jimmy's age. A stranger had come one day to see his mother—a tall man who had suddenly lifted him up off the floor to take a good look at his face. When the man was about to leave, he'd given Jim a nickel.

But Jim's mother had never identified their visitor. She said it was none of his business. His father was dead, she'd tell him. Either that or in jail.

For a while, after the war, Jim had tried to find his father. Since there'd been nothing to keep him in New York—no family ties to speak of, except for Bobby—he took off for the West Coast, hitchhiking a good part of the way, stopping off in a lot of different towns. At each stop he'd get hold of a phone book. There was always a bunch of listings for James Johnson. There were black James Johnsons, white James Johnsons—it had to be one of the commonest names in America. He'd start calling numbers after he'd had enough to drink, asking questions until all his nickels were gone. But he gave up once he got to San Francisco. He checked himself into a rooming house there and stayed drunk for almost a year. That wasn't so unusual for guys like him, he told me. He'd heard the navy had done a study on veterans who'd served on minesweepers and found an unusually high percentage of alcoholics, nervous breakdowns, suicides.

"I know you want to write about me," he said, "but you won't be able to until after I'm gone."

We didn't get married until December—it had taken that long to finalize the divorce. I remember getting out of bed the morning of our wedding to put on the knitted two-piece pale pink outfit I'd just bought. It was a costume I never wore again—it seemed too Upper East Side to go with the conditions of what I thought of as our "real life." There was a hat as well, a beige pillbox number with a floral design on it, which I anchored precariously to my French twist. On our way uptown to the synagogue, we stopped at a florist's near the Spring Street subway station, where Jim bought me a corsage of pale pink rosebuds to go with my dress. Being a bride was a little like going to a prom, I thought giddily, a ritual you had to execute in pastels. I wondered whether we'd feel more "married" than we already were when we lay down together legally later on in the same bed we'd just risen from.

My mother had made the arrangements, found the synagogue where Jim had been going for several weeks of religious instruction by the rabbi who was going to perform the ceremony. I hadn't set foot in a synagogue myself since I was fifteen. I remember feeling abashed by Jim's seriousness about becoming Jewish.

The Rodeph Sholom Congregation was in the West Eighties,

but when the subway stopped at Columbus Circle, Jim suggested we get out there and walk the rest of the way. It was a cold, bright, clear morning. I remember us walking up Broadway arm in arm, exhilarated and a little tense. After a block or two we came to a dark Irish bar bar directly across the street from the Professional Children's School—it must have always been there, but I'd never taken any notice of it during my years as a professional child. Jim said, "We've got plenty of time. Let's have a drink." It was so early the chairs were still up on the tables—we were the only customers. Jim ordered a scotch for himself and champagne for me. After we'd toasted each other, I was afraid he'd want to order another scotch or two, but he didn't. "I only needed one," he said quietly.

The snapshots of our wedding in the rabbi's study are among the few I have in which you can see the two of us together—Jim in the dark suit that originated in Painesville, me all in pink with the pillbox sliding backward on my head and my bangs falling into my eyes. There we are with the rabbi solemnly joining our hands, with my mother and her unchanging expression of smiling through tears, with Bob Whearty and his wife beaming at the two of us—then just Jim and me. He's grabbed me so that the whole side of my body is pressed into his; for that moment even his eyes look happy. We stand at a slant as if the earth is tilting. I smile and hold my breath.

The photographer was Aunt Leona, the self-appointed family historian, with her scrapbooks of my juvenilia and her shoe boxes of snapshots from summer vacations with my mother and Aunt Anna from the Year One and decades of Passover dinners and Uncle Uda's annual visits from Peru, with her flashbulbs popping as her self-conscious subjects tried to remember not to blink. There was such a merciless inevitability to all this ridiculous picture-taking that in my grouchy teens I'd sometimes covered my face and begged Aunt Leona to let me off the hook. Why this passion for commemoration? I used to wonder.

In a notebook I've avoided opening, the gray notebook I bought myself one disconsolate day the following December, when I tried

for a while to put down on paper everything I could manage to remember, I find the following: "The day we were married, we said we'd both had such hard times that maybe God had finally taken pity on us."

I can almost hear Jim saying those words—the voice I can scarcely recognize is my own.

"I'm giving you my name." He said that, too. And it's the one I've kept.

* * *

As a wedding present, my mother gave me a sewing machine. I taught myself to use it. I was going to save money for Jim's canvas and paint by sewing my own clothes. It was the era of the waistless shift dress—just a few seams, and you had a recognizable garment you could pull over your head without requiring a zipper. I remember becoming obsessed with sewing, haunting the notions sections of department stores on my lunch hours to pore over the *Vogue* pattern books, consulting with Martha Apelbaum, the reigning sewing expert in my office, who even made coats and jackets and shirts for her husband, though I didn't think I'd ever get as far as that. On Sundays, when Jim and I took walks on the Lower East Side, we'd stop in at the cut-rate fabric stores on Orchard Street. He took great interest in my sewing, as in everything I did. Sometimes he'd surprise me with fabric he'd bought for me himself. He'd go out to Orchard Street early in the morning right after I went to work—the first customer of the day, he said, always got a special deal. There was a store nearby on Ludlow Street that sold old Jewish books that Jim would also visit. "I'm a better Jew than you are," he'd tease me.

Sometimes I'd come home from the office with my bag of groceries from the A&P near the Spring Street station and discover that Jim had already made dinner. He had two main specialties—lasagna and corned beef and cabbage. He'd make big pots of them—enough to feed us for days. In Painesville, he said, he'd done most of the cooking as well as taking complete care of the kids on the days when his wife was teaching—he could give a hilarious description of the peculiar horror of changing a dirty diaper with a hangover. I always took it as an encouraging sign that Jim had really entered a new phase when he told a funny story about Painesville.

In those days it was still possible to be gracefully poor in New York. Even when we were practically out of money, we could have a good time just by walking around our neighborhood. We could walk down to Chinatown and eat for a dollar in the noodle shops on Mott Street or cross the Bowery at Grand into Little Italy and get coffee gelati at Ferrara's. The side streets were full of secrets—sinister restaurants, basement social clubs, a barbershop where someone "big" had been rubbed out. People we didn't know in Little Italy seemed to know about us. "Ain't you the artist on Chrystie Street?" a man keeping watch on a street corner might say to Jim. "I hear you're all right, and that's good, because this is a quiet neighborhood around here."

Once in Ferrara's we were approached by a middle-aged patron of the arts who wanted Jim to paint a portrait of his girlfriend and announced that he'd be showing up at the studio with her one day very soon. "You don't have to give me the address," he said. "I already got it." When Jim tried to explain that he only did abstract painting, the gentleman remained obtusely insistent. "Every artist knows how to paint a portrait—don't they teach you that in school? I'll make it worth your while—thirty-five dollars. But only if you make her look good."

It was just as well this new relationship never progressed any further. According to Moe, the handsome Italian butcher on our block, the patron of the arts was someone so "important" that it was always advisable to give him exactly what he wanted in order to remain under his proection.

Unfortunately, there was no one to protect us from the housing inspector who rang the bell downstairs one morning while Jim was painting. No sooner had Jim let him in than he condemned the stove, hot-water heater, and refrigerator the sculptor had left us.

That was the worst part of being poor—an unforeseen disaster of this sort could turn into a long setback and remind you how close you always lived to the edge of losing everything you had. It was a reminder Jim couldn't handle. It sent him into a spiral of morose drinking that went on for days, even though I was able to borrow enough money from my mother to replace all the equipment before the inspector's next visit.

It turned bitterly cold that winter. Cold invaded the loft until the cement floor felt like ice. Light entered in different shades of gray. Jim looked around the derelict floor above us—frost covered the smashed pieces of sculpture; there were icicles hanging from the ceiling. We kept the space heater going and ran up a huge gas bill and brought in a potbellied coal stove, despite our fears of the inspector, but we could never seem to get warm. We'd eat dinner hastily and climb up into our bed and wait for the heat of the stove to rise to us. It seemed odd to be living in this manner in New York in 1963. It could have been the winter of 1929, except that we had television. Huddled together under our new red Hudson Bay blanket, we'd watch it for hours, drifting into sleep during the Late Late Movie and hearing "The Star-Spangled Banner" play in our dreams just before the screen went black.

Jim would get up with me in the mornings, and we'd go to Moishe's, the Jewish dairy restaurant on the corner of Grand and the Bowery, and try to warm up over breakfast. Sometimes we'd find bums who'd broken into our downstairs hallway asleep in frozen pools of urine. I'd rush out the door to get away from the smell. Jim would bend over them. Shaking their shoulders, he'd say, "Hey, fellas. You can't stay here." But he'd always feel bad about it. Some of the bums on Grand Street would huddle around fires they'd lit in trash cans. A few of them knew Jim by now. "Yo!" they'd yell as we passed, or even, "Good morning!" One old man who once had a long conversation with Jim had been a cantor in his former life.

After breakfast Jim would wait with me on the Bowery until a Third Avenue bus came along. He'd kiss me good-bye and head back to the studio and put on a pair of woolen gloves with the fingers cut out and try to work. Sometimes he'd tease me by declaring he wasn't going to let me go. "Wait for the next bus," he'd murmur into my ear, or "How about playing hooky with me today?" It was never a plea—he'd always pretend he wasn't serious. But I remember mornings when I was almost afraid to part from him— afraid of what, I didn't exactly know—just afraid for some reason. My fear was like that nameless sound I'd find myself listening for, still far off but coming closer. I had the unreasonable idea he'd be only absolutely safe if I were with him. But if I called in sick too much, I'd lose my job. I'd pay my fare and look out the bus window for a last glimpse of him turning the corner of Grand Street.

The office always seemed amazingly well heated—so much steam, you'd have to open windows. I'd sit at my desk, and soon the fear would begin to fade. I was doing well, everyone told me, definitely going up the ladder—at the rate of about one rung and one dollar at a time. People didn't yet believe young women really lived on what they earned. Still, no one ever asked me to type a letter anymore. Instead I was given the manuscripts no one else wanted to edit—the annual updated edition of *Fielding's Travel Guide* and the Peter Field Westerns.

Temple Fielding believed the discerning traveler should always travel with a folded one-hundred-dollar bill in an inside pocket of his bespoke suit; he wrote with loathing of places like Albania and Bulgaria and once accused me of trying to make him sound like Hemingway.

Peter Field's favorite word was *scree*. Due to their dearth of female characters, his books were sold in bulk to the armed forces as wholesome reading for young men. There were four Peter Fields a year. The terrain was always full of rocks and treacherous ravines and mountainsides where scree abounded. Bits of scree would fly through the air during gun battles, or men would have to crawl through it on their bellies on their way to shelter behind various escarpments. There seemed to be no actual Peter Field—just the neat typescripts, each exactly 220 pages, that arrived in the mail like clockwork, over which I now had been entrusted with total control through each stage of production. It would have been a cinch, Jim and I once decided, to substitute a wild avant-garde work of the same length and publish it as a Peter Field under a title such as *Redstone Shootout.* Maybe it would be months before the switch was detected.

Sometimes I'd call Jim to read him a choice passage from the page in front of me—at least, that was the ostensible reason. Sometimes he'd be the one who phoned first—"Just checking in," he'd say, as if he'd read my mind. "It's getting too cold here. I think I'll go uptown for a while."

"Uptown" could mean either of two places—a bar called Dillon's, frequented by displaced habitués of the Cedar, which had shocked the art world by closing that fall and hadn't yet reopened in a new location, or McSorley's Alehouse on Seventh Street just off the Bowery. McSorley's was a relic of old New York that still had most of its original fittings, even gaslight fixtures and the old white tiles on its sawdust-covered floor. Its potbellied stove was a holy icon.

Wives whose husbands became regulars at McSorley's supposedly had little to worry their pretty heads about. If their men stag-

gered home, it was just from drinking ale (which was even recommended, in those days, as a tonic during pregnancy). Hanging out
at McSorley's also increased the odds that a man would stay faith-
ful, since no women whatsoever—neither mates nor predators—
were allowed on the premises. If you absolutely had to, you could
reach your man by phone, hanging on as you listened to a pro-
longed undersea roar, which rose to hilarious heights after the bartender's humiliating shout: "Jim! Yer old lady!" Beloved customers
who occasionally couldn't make it home on their own unreliable
feet were tenderly put to bed in a back room. By that winter Jim
had established himself there.

The hours Jim spent in McSorley's seemed to fold up on him like
an accordion. It would be three in the afternoon; then it would
suddenly be eight. He'd get up to leave and be stunned to step
outside into starless darkness. Meanwhile I'd be down on Chrystie
Street, trying to keep the dinner warm and waiting for the phone
to ring. Finally he'd call me from somewhere.

"I'm on Rivington on my way downtown. In a phone booth. I
always come home to you, don't I, baby? I always come home—
you know that's true."

I think now of his first wife using up her nights doing crossword puzzles at the kitchen table in Painesville when Jim was out
in the Volvo. On my kitchen table it was sewing. When Jim came
in, it wouldn't even look like I'd been waiting, just working on another dress. "I had to turn the oven off," was all I'd say. Unless I'd
been feeling scared because he was much later than usual.

He'd take one look at my face. "What's the matter with you?"

"I just wish you'd called me earlier."

"It isn't women, if that's what's bothering you."

"What is it then?"

But if we went on from there, we could end up in the places I dreaded to go.

"Look—I'd give you the last drop of blood in my body if you needed it."

"I'm not asking for the last drop of blood."

Once he said to me very sadly, "I'll only leave you one time."

"What is that supposed to mean?" I yelled at him. But he wouldn't tell me.

I remember him bringing home from McSorley's a small container of their famous concoction of cheddar cheese and onions, so that even though I could never cross the threshold, I could taste what it was like to be there. "They know who I am," he'd say.

Whenever he'd gone to the Cedar, the thought that none of the New York painters had ever seen his work had eaten away at him. To them he'd been just another new face—a Johnny-come-lately who hadn't been around when it counted. At McSorley's he didn't have to prove anything. He could just come in, order a drink and find people he could talk to—"guys from all walks of life." And if he didn't feel like talking—if his mind was still wrestling with a painting he'd had to walk away from—that would be accepted, too.

One celebrity showed up—Brendan Behan, who was not only a world-famous writer but a world-famous drunk. Behan was alone, so Jim walked up to him and stuck out his hand. "I'm James Johnson—an American painter."

"I don't know you," Behan said.

In the gray notebook I find only one mention of Bob Reardon, although he became a fixture in our lives after he and Jim met at McSorley's. I remember Reardon was a war veteran. He'd fought in Italy, he and Jim had that in common—that and their Irish blood and the disaffected feeling McSorley's ale seemed to bring to the surface that the greatness that was in them might never be made known to the world. Reardon had been writing a novel forever; hundreds of pages, maybe thousands, had been piling up since he'd gotten out of the service. No one but his wife had read them.

At McSorley's, Reardon's book was rumored to be The Great American Novel. He checked in there every day of the week, as if reporting to a job. His drinking would proceed inexorably at a measured pace; when he finished at the bar, he'd continue at home. The regulars shook their heads over the condition of his liver.

The first time I saw Reardon, I thought he was in his sixties, but he couldn't have been more than forty-five. I remember his portly torso and uneven gait and the lock of gray hair that flopped boyishly into one eye. He still had the raddled remains of Irish good looks.

I soon began to think we were spending far too many Saturday nights with the Reardons. We had the honor of being the only couple they cared to entertain. They'd evidently been lonely, before Jim and I came along, in the apartment they said was a "fabulous deal." The Reardons occupied the entire second floor of an old brick building on Second Avenue next to an Italian funeral parlor. They'd buzz us in, and their inner sanctum would close around us, with its teetering piles of books and papers and the glasses Reardon had drained and forgotten and the overstuffed armchairs with shredded upholstery that seemed to sag the way Reardon did. The shredder was a huge gray-and-white cat, who would jump on my lap and settle there, ignoring the pellets of dried food Reardon would shy in its direction from time to time— "Billy! Want a treat?" he'd call in vain.

I'd keep petting the cat, hoping I could pass for a good listener, as I wondered how many hours it would be before Jim would be willing to go home. Maybe that's why I can't recall any of the profundities about literature and life Reardon uttered from the wrecked throne in which he always installed himself—only the alarming way he'd have to heave himself out of it every time he had to journey to the bathroom and the despairing look on his wife's face as she brought in more beers from the refrigerator and her surprising prickly loyalty to Reardon, the way it encircled him like a hedge of thorns.

Sometimes when we were with the Reardons, I'd catch reflected glimpses of Jim and me—down the road in ten years' time. But Jim, I'd tell myself, wasn't an alcoholic. He was still a grieving man—more time was all he needed. There were even days he didn't need to drink at all.

"Oh Joyce, death was after him so bad." That was the sentence of Reardon's I preserved in the notebook. I knew I'd have a whole life in which to think about it.

The approaching sound can be identified now. The metallic stutter of an old red motorcycle—not quite regular—with a hesitation every now and then. If you were really listening very hard for it— if you'd shut off the radio and the sewing machine—you could sometimes hear its tinny staccato even blocks away against the rush and hum of the traffic proceeding downtown, passing the corner of Grand and the Bowery, where Jim would always say to cab-drivers, "Make the light." The sound would get louder as the machine triumphantly made its left turn. It would rise to a crescendo downstairs just below the front windows; then abruptly there'd be silence until I heard the street door open and close.

We called it The Bike. It was the Harley 220 Jim bought himself that spring, for which he paid the previous owner two hundred and fifty dollars. The bike was low-powered compared to the models you might associate with the Hell's Angels, but it could take you places. And that was the whole point, as Jim often said.

He'd been complaining of feeling cooped up in the city, especially now that the weather was getting good. "I've always had wheels," he'd say, still looking wistful each time he saw a gray

Volvo. He said there was nothing like complete freedom of movement. The craving for wheels was in his blood, something he'd inherited from his old man. Maybe he decided to get the bike
because freedom of movement, unlike other things he'd lost,
could be recaptured. Or because he identified with Robert Wray, a
tall, lanky, fatherless nineteen-year-old from Texas, who'd run off
to New York to be a painter and turned up at McSorley's.

Robert Wray was a waif with a talent for getting himself
adopted—already he'd landed a job stretching canvases for de
Kooning—and he could hold his own in Jim's crowd, although the
regulars at McSorley's teased him about the wispy blond mustache
he'd grown in order to appear older and wiser. He'd had a Harley
in Texas that he'd swapped for a pickup truck when he headed
north, but he still missed his bike. "It's just your ass goin' down
the middle of the road," I remember him saying to us one night
when Jim brought him home for lasagna. It didn't sound very ap-
pealing to me, but Jim laughed and said he liked that idea and that
all the painting he did was that way too.

About a week later, I came home from work, and there was the
red bike out on the sidewalk and the two of them going over it,
their hands black with grease, very pleased with themselves for
spotting the ad in the paper. Moe the butcher and a couple of
men from the auto repair place next door were looking on, giving
advice.

I remember a lot of light in the evening sky—it must have been
May by then—and Jim insisting that he take me for a spin as soon
as I put the groceries away, and Robert Wray assuring me that Jim
could already operate the bike as if he'd been raised in Texas. I remember warily getting on the thing, holding on to Jim for dear life
as we bumped over the cobblestoned streets in our neighborhood.

It took me a while to learn to be a good passenger, but I did get the hang of it. You couldn't be stiff and fearful and offer resistance—you had to sway the way the bike wanted you to, as I'd had to learn to sway with Jim. Soon the bike almost seemed like a great idea—the very thing that had been missing from our lives, and we'd never even realized it.

On weekend mornings we'd get up as soon as it was light and head out of the city before the Long Island Expressway crowded up, looking for a beach where Jim could fish. We'd fly along in the stiff wind the bike generated, cold air rushing under our nylon jackets, chilling our faces, while everything around us baked and gleamed in the sun. I'd be wound around Jim on the buddy seat, my knees pressed against his thighs, shutting my eyes whenever we went down "death alley" between two lanes of slower-moving cars. The fear was part of the pleasure, though—I understood that about the bike. And after the first few trips, I could keep my eyes open and tell my arms to unclench, to hold Jim more loosely, though I couldn't help looking out for the things, besides my fear, that could do us in—a patch of sand or gravel just ahead, an iridescent spill of oil, a bump on the road surface. It was a heightened kind of consciousness the bike thrust upon you. Sometimes I even thought it wouldn't be so bad if we died one day while we were out there flying along. We'd be going around a curve a little too fast, and the sun would be in our eyes; the last thing I'd see would be the brown back of Jim's neck and then—nothing. How could you be afraid of nothing?

I think I could allow myself to be open to such thoughts because alongside any fear I had of the bike was my eerie certainty that out on those roads Jim would never let anything bad happen to me—

and that because of this he would never be in danger as long as I was riding on the seat behind him. But most of the time he was on the bike alone.

He'd go for rides after he finished working, and the rides had a way of ending up at McSorley's, though at first he didn't stay there nearly as late as he used to. In fact, he almost convinced me—because I badly wanted to be convinced—that having the bike was going to cure him of drinking. He'd never get on that thing drunk, he swore. I wanted him to promise me that. "Promises are for children," he said—not angrily, just reminding me to back off, not to turn myself into a nagging woman.

That summer Jim seemed to be putting a little world together for himself. He'd met another young painter at McSorley's whom he enjoyed taking under his wing. Pete Leventhal was older, though, than Robert Wray, in his late twenties. He'd done all sorts of adventurous things to make a living, including working on a clamming boat in Northport, Long Island. Jim loved hearing about the clammers, who, according to Pete, were a die-hard breed of rugged individualists and hard drinkers—he made Northport sound like the Wild West.

I always felt funny hearing about Northport; for me it had different—and painful—associations. Kerouac had retreated to that town with his mother in the summer of '58, when his notoriety was beginning to make him reclusive and paranoid. Even though I learned from Pete that Kerouac and his mother had recently moved elsewhere, I still regarded Northport as the place that had swallowed him up, because Jack had never really come back from there, as far as I was concerned.

I had a sorrowful soft spot for Kerouac. I could never have stayed with Jack—I knew that by then—his drinking alone would have driven me away. But there were people you didn't stop caring

about even when they went out of your life—people who couldn't
help hurting you because of what they did to themselves. There
were things about Jim that reminded me of Jack—his intensity, his
awareness of mortality, his single-minded passion for his work.
But Jack had a deadly void in his heart—he could only put the love
that was in him into his writing; whoever he was with, he'd be
profoundly alone. Rightly or wrongly, I believed that was the main
reason Kerouac would never stop drinking. But Jim, I told myself,
despite everything that had been done to him, had a limitless capacity for love.

We went out to Northport finally one Saturday when Pete Leventhal was there because Jim had to see it for himself. We sat on
the town pier for hours watching sails bobbing far out on the bay
that opened into Long Island Sound, and we saw the clammers
come in, their small open boats laden with bulging burlap bags
that looked as though they were filled with wet stones. It was a
desperate business, clamming, Pete said—you went out alone and
never knew what kind of luck you'd have, how much you'd be
able to bring back. Clammers, I soon noticed, drank even more
than painters. In the waterfront bar Pete took us to, the air sim-
mered with incipient fights about territory in the bay or women,
and just as we were about to leave, a couple of men picked up the
jukebox and threw it out on the sidewalk. We stepped over shards
of glass and smashed .45s as we made our way out of there.

That night we slept belowdecks on someone's boat. Soon after
we woke up, Jim caught some flounder, and we got on the bike
and found a beach where we could gather wood and make a fire,
and we ate the fish for breakfast. I remember we talked excitedly
about an idea Pete Leventhal had suggested to us—about buying
an old fishing vessel in Nova Scotia, sailing it down the coast, and
living on it every summer even after we got around to having kids.

After that first trip, Jim wanted to go back to Northport. In August we spent several days of my vacation there in a boarding-house, but his mood had darkened by then, and we started having fights about how much he was drinking nightly and my lack of fascination with the clammers' bar and my unwillingness to set foot in it. He'd head there himself on the bike after I'd gone to bed, and I'd lie awake in anguish, wondering if I should have gone with him, until I heard the familiar stutter just outside in the small hours of the morning and knew he'd proved once again that I'd made myself miserable for nothing.

We were visited late in the summer by two self-appointed emissaries from Painesville. Doug Brownell was an up-and-coming businessman—he was in something like machine parts or cement. The restlessness of his wife, Linda, had led her to dabble in the arts. She presented me with a bulbous brown ceramic ashtray she'd made for us as a belated wedding present, which Doug said gave him an excuse to "kiss the bride." He handed Jim a quart of scotch and made known his desire for a "real party."

"I'm not much into parties," Jim said. "I've taken up living."

"Well, it shows, darlin'," Linda shrieked, and she walked over to him and squeezed his shoulders and gave him an approximation of a soulful look, which he did not return.

The Brownells had come to New York with orchestra seats for the latest Broadway shows, but I suspected we were the main attraction. Linda swore there hadn't been anything really juicy to talk about in Painesville since Jim had left town—"I don't even go to art workshop anymore. It just isn't the same."

She had a pug nose and little round brown eyes, and she kept avidly taking in our household arrangements, looking everywhere

except at me, and even demanded a ride on the motorcycle—
"Can't we just go around the corner or somethin, darlin'?"

"Go ahead," Doug said impassively, filling his glass again with
scotch.

Their repartee seemed loaded with double meanings, and later,
after the Brownells had left, Jim told me he'd gone to bed with
Linda once or twice in one crazy period and could never figure out
whether or not Doug knew or cared.

When they'd called up out of the blue, he hadn't really wanted
to see them, but he'd accepted a lot of their hospitality in
Painesville. The Brownells were rich, he told me, and had bought a
painting from his last show; maybe now he could get them to buy
another. "How would you like to go home with one of the first
paintings I've done in New York?" he asked them.

The Brownells said that would be really exciting, and wouldn't
it prove to all concerned that nothing could stop Jim Johnson?
They went into the studio with Jim and picked out the largest
painting there, which they said they'd buy on the installment plan.
Doug whipped out his ballpoint to write a check for a small down
payment. But they never sent the rest of the money.

They asked Jim if he was up for some gossip, not that they had
much to tell him.

"Yeah, you might as well give it to me," Jim said grimly.

It was trivial stuff, more or less—no stories, just details of daily
life. Jim's ex had traded in the Volvo and bought herself a new red
car and had been seen by Linda with some blond streaks in her
hair. And someone who had visited the house said Jim's paintings
were hanging all over the place and had noticed that his son Bobby
was now riding a tricycle. Jimmy had started school, but was said
to be having a little trouble.

"Well, I'm afraid that's it," said Linda.

"And it ain't much," Doug chimed in.

"The pain's the same," said Jim.

The Brownells were the couple he had been visiting his last night in Painesville when he almost crashed the Volvo. They still remembered peering out their frosted-up dining room window, watching him stumble to the car through the snowdrifts that covered the driveway.

"We just laughed and laughed," Linda said.

Fall came, but the summer hung on. The days were pallid and warm, and as October ended, bums were still sleeping in the park across the way under the plane trees that seemed to feel no impetus to shed their leaves. The previous fall, I'd watched them turn gold; this time they just looked leaden, weighted each day with a little more dust. I remember hoping for signs of winter. I didn't even dread the freezing weather, the weeks when it would be too cold for us to do anything but climb up into bed—too cold for Jim to go anywhere on the bike.

We were still riding out to Sheepshead Bay on weekends with extra sweaters under our jackets—outings like that seemed to save us, remind us of our old feeling of being profoundly together. But trouble would come when the week began again, when I had to leave Jim to go to my job. Not long after the Brownells' visit, he had stopped painting. The last few canvases he'd been working on had been entirely without color—massive black forms crowding out the white. He couldn't stand to look at those paintings—they were definitely going to end up on the floor. He said he realized how much of his development depended on his sense of continuity—without that, how could he know what he was doing?

He took the bike uptown much earlier now and came home on it much later. I'd call the studio when I came back from lunch, hoping to find him there, but he never was. I'd sit at my desk in a panic, holding myself back from calling McSorley's or the Cedar, which had just reopened a few blocks from its original location with a new self-conscious rough-hewn decor. Some days I couldn't bear to go home right after work; instead I'd look for someone to have coffee with, or I'd kill a couple of hours in department stores trying on clothes I couldn't afford.

Kerouac unexpectedly turned up that fall. I had just walked into the loft one evening in October and had run over to the ringing phone, expecting to speak with Jim, but the low melodic voice with the slightly flattened *a*'s on the other end was unmistakable, even after four years. Jack hadn't called me since we'd broken up, and I couldn't imagine how he'd found my number, but he said he was in New York for a couple of days—he and his mother had just sold their house in Florida and moved back to Northport. He was staying with his friend Lucien Carr in the Village and wanted me to come right over and join them—it was as if no time had passed at all, as if Jack walked around in such a state of obliviousness that it never occurred to him he might not find me exactly where he remembered leaving me. "You know, I'm married now," I told him. He didn't ask for any details. "Just bring your little husband," he said.

I didn't think Jim would agree to go. He still got touchy when he was reminded of the men in my past—as if I should have waited for him, as if he had the impossible wish to recast my life as well as his own. And these days there was no telling what might set off his anger. To my surprise, though, he said he knew this was important to me, and so he'd take me to see Jack after dinner.

Jack and Lucien had been drinking for hours by the time we arrived. Jack registered that I was there, but seemed to have forgotten whatever impulse it was that had made him want to summon me. Under their film of bleary sadness, his eyes were the same blue I remembered, but his body was thick now, his belly bulged against his shirt, his face was reddened by broken blood vessels. It was horrifying to see what four more years of drinking had done to him. When Jack and Lucien started yelling at each other and stabbing each other with the lighted ends of their cigarettes, Jim gave me a look that said, Had enough? and we left. I never saw Jack again.

I open the gray notebook at random, and Jim says, "You'll survive me." We'd been in the midst of a conversation about how Cézanne died—painting in a rainstorm. "No!" I hear myself protest. "You'll be an old man like Matisse."

Our voices rise from the pages as if they'd been shut up in there.

"You think you're special, don't you?" he says bitterly one night when we've been fighting. "You're a very special person."

"No, I'm not."

"But you think you are. You're hard."

"Please—let's just go back to sleep."

All our fights that fall were about the same thing—my need to know that he was safe, my desperate insistence on getting him home—"one more time," as he'd put it, mockingly or with a tone of weary resignation. "I never ask you for anything, do I?"

He was never the one to call from McSorley's at ten or eleven and tell me to find a taxi and come get him. It would be Pete Leventhal or Robert Wray or the bartender or even Reardon who would realize as Jim was trying to leave that he was in no condition to get on the bike. Jim would laugh incredulously or get furious when they pleaded with him to just leave the damn bike parked outside; sometimes they'd have to pick his pocket and take his keys away. "We have the keys—don't worry," they'd say to me when they called.

He outfoxed them all one night before I could get there and started walking home down the Bowery. The police were out in full force, sweeping through the neighborhood, throwing all the drunks into paddy wagons. They stopped Jim on Rivington Street and only let him go after he took out his wallet and found something in it that proved he had an address. "You see how easy it would be just to merge into all that," he said to me later in wonderment. "You see how easy it would be, don't you?"

It was always a humiliating struggle to get him into the taxi that had brought me, and sometimes I had no idea how I'd make him come upstairs. I remember us yelling at each other once because he wanted me to stand on Chrystie Street looking at the moon with him, and I wouldn't. I ran into the house by myself and then came down to see if he was still there. "Why do you always want me to come upstairs with you?" he asked me. "What are you afraid of?" I remember lying, saying I didn't know.

In one of the quarrels written down in the notebook, I shout at him, "Why do you pick on me all the time—yes, all the time—for no reason. You're making me hate you!"

He takes his wallet and throws it down on the street and walks away from me. As he reaches the end of the block, I hear him yelling, "I'm asking God to strike me down!"

Once I left him after we were halfway up the stairs. I ran down and opened the street door. There was nothing out there and no place I wanted to be except with him.

"Can you stand it?" he asks me in the notebook.

"Yes, I can stand it."

"But it's expensive. All valuable things are expensive."

In November, when it began to get colder but still not too cold to ride the bike, Jim suddenly began cutting down on his drinking and his visits to McSorley's. We were gentle with each other, a little tentative, exhausted, as if we'd just barely survived an enormous storm. He still wasn't painting, but he'd found jobs for himself and Robert Wray directly across the park.

Milton Resnick, a relatively obscure abstract expressionist in his sixties, had just had a wildly successful show, despite the fact that pop art, which seemed to us a ridiculously lightweight kind of painting, was beginning to receive a lot of attention. Temporarily rich for the first time in his life, Resnick had bought an abandoned synagogue on Forsyth Street and needed carpenters to turn it into the magnificent studio he had always dreamed of. Maybe it was the daily work for Resnick that began to steady Jim; maybe it was knowing that nothing we had gone through together had wrenched us apart.

I remember a nighttime walk along Broadway—one of the last walks we took. In those days, that stretch of Lower Manhattan was a ghost town after dark, once the factories and offices closed. As we were making our way back uptown, we noticed an empty mailbag left out on the sidewalk. "You know something"—Jim stooped to get a look at it—"this is great canvas. Pure linen. Just feel how heavy it is." We decided to take it home. It seemed lucky, that gift from the streets—a message that it was time for Jim to start painting again.

He borrowed my sewing shears to cut up the bag, then searched the studio until he found a tube that still had a few remaining drops of cadmium red. Before we went to bed, he made three small perfect paintings, each with only a couple of quick, broad, briefly considered strokes that seemed to suggest continuing showers of black and red beyond the frayed margins of the canvas.

He got up early the next morning to see what he thought of those little paintings and wouldn't let me make breakfast until I'd looked at them again, too. Grabbing me by the shoulders, he said, "Don't you see, kiddo! Small can be large!"

He could feel he was on the verge of a turning point in the way he worked. In fact, he said, the past months had been like the period after he stopped doing watercolors. He'd broken the watercolor brushes and thrown the paints away, then spent a terrible year struggling with oils, painting out the image. Now he was going to go for something much harder than what he'd arrived at before he came to New York—he was going to work with color the way Japanese *sumi* masters had with ink, only on a grand scale, so the size of the strokes would be in proportion to the size of the canvas. The only thing that could hold him back was that there weren't brushes big enough for what he realized he was finally ready to do, but somehow he'd find a way around that.

Several days later we were in Little Italy together, walking home with bags of groceries. It wasn't long before Thanksgiving—workmen were up on rooftops stringing wires of colored lights over Grand Street. Suddenly I felt Jim tap my arm. "Look up!" I looked up just as a pigeon flew into a wire that twisted around its neck.

We stared at the bedraggled gray bundle of feathers dangling above Grand Street. "Just think," Jim said to me, "that bird had the whole fucking sky to fly in."

* * *

On Friday, November 22, we watched television all night—the unbelievable unfolding news, the anguished interviews, the details of the investigation so far. What had happened to John F. Kennedy earlier that day reminded Jim of the bird—the way all the circumstances had converged in a single instant, the fine weather, the open car, the hand and eye of the assassin, the president's stiff-necked insistence on appearing in Dallas despite the warnings of danger. There it was, he said almost with awe—the same lesson brought home to him over and over. Because I stayed silent, he said to me, "You haven't learned this yet. You don't even want to think about it."

I was only *pretending* I didn't think about it. Nothing could have made me reveal the superstitious dread inside me. Owning up to what I feared might make it real.

The relentless notebook records an exchange we had about the bike.

"Do you want me to get rid of it?" he asks me.

I answer, "No, I just want you to be careful."

"Because I was afraid of losing him," I wrote a month later, "afraid he would love me less."

Thanksgiving was a day of thick gray light, still unseasonably warm. The grayness seeped into me as I chopped onions and boiled sweet potatoes and read the directions for making pumpkin pie. I was making dinner for just the two of us and had been looking forward to it, but suddenly all the cutting and chopping and preparation seemed futile. I felt profoundly alone with my concealed apprehensiveness, my inescapable sense that doom was about to overtake us.

I was about to light the oven when Jim put on the black down jacket I'd just bought him and announced he was going to make a quick run on the bike to try and find Robert Wray and bring him home to have turkey with us. Robert Wray didn't have a phone, but Jim knew where he lived and was also going to look for him at McSorley's; he doubted the kid had been invited anywhere for Thanksgiving.

Panic leapt through me as I listened. "I'd rather you didn't," I found myself saying.

Jim didn't know what to make of my reaction. There was plenty of food, he pointed out, too much food, in fact—we'd

still be eating leftovers next week. And wasn't it sad—wasn't it
selfish—not to share all that food with a friend?

"I just don't want Robert here today," I kept insisting, even
though I would have been glad to see him if he'd appeared at our
door—or to see anyone else we knew. The truth was, I would have
said anything to keep Jim off the bike that afternoon because I
was convinced, for no reason, he'd have a terrible accident if I let
him go.

He finally tore off his jacket and disappeared into his studio,
slamming the door behind him. He was still too angry to speak to
me by the time I put the turkey on the table. We drank our wine
and ate as the television continued its doleful replays of Kennedy's
funeral, its shots of the president's young widow, stoic in black, his
small boy saluting as his father's coffin passed.

I'd ruined Thanksgiving, but I'd kept him alive one more day.

By the next morning he'd forgiven me. He'd been lying awake
thinking how jittery I'd seemed, not only yesterday but for weeks.
The drinking was hurting us, he said, and so he was going to stop
it altogether—or at least try. Maybe he wouldn't need to drink
right now, because his mind was on the work he was about to do,
not on the things that hurt him that couldn't be helped. Yes, he
was going to quit and see what it felt like.

I burst into tears, and he held me and murmured, "You don't
know whether you're laughing or crying," which was what he always said when we made up after a fight. "This time you should be
laughing because you're getting something you want."

"Oh, I'm laughing all right," I sobbed into his chest.

"Yeah? I don't think so." He was stroking my hair. "Not yet
anyway."

\* \* \*

He spent the weekend cleaning up his studio, clearing a wall of the black, claustrophobic paintings he hadn't signed his name to and putting up a new piece of canvas, six feet high, which he began sizing with gesso. I could hear a Lightnin' Hopkins record Robert Wray had lent him playing as he worked—it had a song Jim was crazy about called "Last Night Blues," and he'd always stop the record player after he'd listened to it once and put the needle back in place and play it one more time. The canvas stayed on the wall all week without a brush mark on it. He'd go into the studio, put the record on again, light a cigarette, and sit on a milk crate, his eyes fixed on that pristine white field stretched out in front of him.

He talked with excitement, the night Robert Wray and Pete Leventhal came over to eat leftover turkey with us, about all the experiments he was planning—lashing different bunches of brushes together or maybe even trying to work with a broom. He'd have to put all that off for a while, though, until he'd saved enough money to buy acrylics in large quantities. When his two friends said they'd been surprised not to see him at McSorley's, he said, "Yeah, well, I'm trying to stop the booze."

Pete Leventhal said he'd been awfully broke. Fortunately, he was about to make two hundred and fifty dollars because he'd just gotten a commission to do a mural for some bar in Brooklyn. The only problem was, he didn't know how he'd be able to work on it in his small apartment. "You can do it here," Jim immediately offered. "I'll clear out one day, so that you can have the place to yourself and get a good start."

They settled on the following Monday, December 9.

A convergence was beginning to take shape, but no one was aware of it, not even me, because I was happier that first week in

December than I'd been for a long time. I even almost stopped listening for that sound in the distance when Jim was off somewhere on the bike.

It felt strange to be living without fear, to remember it but not feel it when we said good-bye on the Bowery in the mornings. "See you later," he'd say with a quick kiss as the bus slowed to a stop and opened its doors, and I'd know he'd walk across the park to his job and that I'd find him waiting by the time I got home and that he'd tell me he'd gotten through one more day without a drink, each day a victory, a sign that we were going to make it in spite of everything—in spite of the past, in spite of setbacks, in spite of the unexpected difficulties life kept throwing our way, like the landlord knocking on our door one evening that same week to inform us we'd probably have to be moving out because the housing inspector had filed a complaint against the building and the trouble of keeping us wasn't worth it to him.

As the landlord went down the stairs, Jim shouted after him, "They'll have to carry us out of here!" But then he turned and put his arms around me and said we'd always be together wherever we went, and even the threat that we might lose the loft couldn't entirely penetrate the strange calm that seemed to have wrapped itself around us.

As if loose ends were being rapidly tied up those last few days in a denouement suddenly underway, Jim saw his mother and his stepfather one more time. The stepfather had been rushed by ambulance to a hospital in the Bronx, where his right leg was amputated—Jim's mother was there with him. It was Bob Whearty who called that night and told Jim, apologizing for disturbing us, saying he'd understand if Jim didn't want to come. "Bobby needs me," Jim said, putting on his jacket and rushing off.

He returned exhausted and silent hours later with a bulky package in a brown paper bag, which he threw into a corner. He didn't tell me until the morning that his mother had made him take his stepfather's shoes. "You always asked me for shoes, didn't you?" she'd said to him.

When we went out to have breakfast, we took them with us, left them for the bums on top of a garbage can on Grand Street.

We stayed in most of that weekend—didn't feel like going anywhere. By now the landlord's threat was weighing upon us, though we weren't talking yet about what to do, where to get the money for a new loft. I remember looking up as I stood at the kitchen counter slicing an onion for dinner and thinking how beautiful the place was.

The television was on. Jim was lying on the couch watching *Victory at Sea*. He'd been watching the old black-and-white World War II footage all day. The whole series was being rebroadcast, and now there was a segment about Anzio. Suddenly I heard him shout, "There's my goddamn ship! Come and see my ship!" But I remained rooted to where I was standing a second too long.

After dinner we saw the final episodes together—the shots of young men pouring off the ships at the end of the war, waiting crowds screaming with joy, waving like crazy, leaping upon the men who had returned. Tears ran down Jim's face. "No one was waiting for me," he said.

"Why didn't I want to look at his ship on TV?" I asked myself in the notebook. I'll never be able to account for that.

* * *

"The last time he painted," I wrote. "The sounds of the paint hitting the canvas—like the flight of a great bird over all the stupid conversation with Robert Wray and the artist from Texas who wanted to 'get pointers.' 'Don't go in there,' I told them.

"His laugh of triumph. I went in first and saw the red and

brown forms that nearly filled the canvas, joined by one wide transparent stroke.

" 'Know what that is, kiddo? You and me walking down Orchard Street.'

"I kissed him and got paint all over my face and said I didn't care. I washed the paint off his face with oil. There was paint caked in his hair. His hands were covered with paint which wouldn't come off, which hadn't washed off even by Monday. 'Do you see me?' he said. 'I think you see me.' "

\* \* \*

About the last day, I wrote nothing down. Because all the details had fused themselves to me, and I couldn't bear to make sense of them. Later I'd go over and over the same ground, looking for clues to what he might have been thinking, to what had made him let go of the handlebars, suddenly, around three P.M. at the corner of Grand and the Bowery when he must have been nearly ready to make the turn. Was it only a question of inches, of the yellow Ryder truck there in front of him stopping short before he could put his foot on the brake? Someone saw him rise up on the seat before he fell. It had just started to snow, and he was almost home. He lay in the street until the ambulance came and was able to tell the driver his name was James Johnson.

The diner around the corner, Moishe's—where we used to eat breakfast before our partings on weekday mornings—vanished along with the entire Boulevard of Cut-rate Brides when the neighborhood went Chinese, like the stage set of a play that had closed after a long run. After December 9, 1963, I never walked in there again anyhow, afraid of running into our ghosts in the booth just behind the cashier with its excellent view of the corner of Grand and the Bowery, where even a day afterward there wasn't a trace of what had happened, not the slightest groove in the asphalt.

Moishe's had a short-order cook who played his transistor radio behind the counter, and I remember the big news on December 9, that Frank Sinatra's son had been kidnapped, followed by a rendition by Sinatra's daughter Nancy of "These Boots Are Meant for Walking," then an announcer saying with due solemnity, "Today is the first day of Chanukah, the Jewish Festival of Lights."

"I feel full of light," Jim said with something in his voice that took me by surprise, something I can only describe now as a kind of contained elation. Aside from that, it appeared to be an ordinary Monday.

He put me on the bus as usual, after we let the first one go by, but the second inevitably came. And that was it—the last time we looked at each other, the last time we touched and kissed. The end of all that.

The next time I saw him, he was stretched out on a marble slab in the morgue, still wearing his navy blue sweater, his black down jacket. His brown hair was the only part of him that seemed alive.

An ordinary Monday. I rejected manuscripts, had a later lunch than usual with women from the office, returned around two just as the phone on my desk was ringing. It was Jim.

"Just checking in. I wanted you to know where I was." His voice still had that quiet, elated tone.

He'd stopped in at the Cedar Bar after leaving Resnick's place because Pete Leventhal was still in the studio, working on his mural.

He must have sensed I was disappointed to hear he was at the Cedar. Very gently, he told me I had nothing to worry about. He'd ordered one beer, but only took a few sips before he left the glass on the bar and walked away. Now he was heading down to Chrystie Street to shave and put on his suit because that night we were going to have dinner with my mother—my foolish mother, whom we always had to dress up for, who could never just take us as we came, she was part of the equation, just as I was. "I'll be outside at five," he told me.

At four I noticed it was snowing a little and was glad I'd had the foresight to keep an umbrella in the office.

At five I went down in the elevator and didn't find him, though I knew he'd be along any minute. I put up the umbrella and waited in front of the building. It was dark by then and much colder than it had been when I went out to lunch. Gusts of snow came down in big wet flakes, in white shafts under the streetlamps. People kept their heads down and hurried to the subways.

By six, lights were going out in the office building across the street. I'd begun making calls by then, but it was hours since anyone had seen Jim. Pete had worked in the studio till four-thirty and left. Every few minutes I called our number and heard the phone ringing.

It was all terribly familiar to me, the way I had imagined this awful kind of waiting, the way I'd felt sometimes when Jim was at McSorley's—until the bartender found him and I could allow myself to be angry because I'd been so afraid for no reason. I'd always thought I'd be waiting at home because I knew he'd never keep me waiting on a street corner. But I'd never really believed the unthinkable could happen.

Finally I hailed a cab because I had to see if the bike was parked on Chrystie Street. "Chrystie Street?" said the driver. "I never heard of it."

When I got out of the cab, I saw that the three guys who worked in the auto repair shop next door to us were standing out on the sidewalk. They stared at me, then looked away, as if they were embarrassed. I shouted at them.

"Something's happened!"

Finally, one of them said, "Oh, honey, you'd better go upstairs . . ."

*I never found transcendence, but I did stay in motion.*
    *In some sense I haven't gone on to that distance they say you can get*

*to through the act of putting words down on paper—promised to take you "beyond" like that anodyne given women after birth, so their bodies won't remember the agonies of labor.*

*But what of the incurables? Those who keep circling back to the same places, always in peril of foundering on avoidance, as time itself turns everything into fiction?*

*He said this to me once—it's in the notebook—*
  *"I will leave my traces."*

# THREE

# Negative Space

*That first week of September there was different air. The sky turned a blue unmitigated by clouds with a deeper undercoat of gray. Light spilled upon the fading garden, gilding the leaves that had suddenly gone dry, glorifying the browning ferns, making each red or purple or cadmium yellow stark and definite. It was warm enough in Vermont to sit on the porch, and I remember how often my thoughts turned to Peter when I was out there—Peter on his porch in the Catskills in the tiny house he'd sent me pictures of in July. I'd imagine him sitting there transfixed by the light, watching it brighten, darken, brighten. All that week, in a curious way, he seemed present, soundlessly very near me. Perhaps that was the reason I lost track of the fact he was supposed to be back in New York. As the days passed without a call from him, it didn't occur to me to wonder why.*

*We were still legally, and in other senses, married, even though we had not lived together for thirty years. Peter had remained in the loft on Greene Street from which I'd abruptly exited in 1971, taking our five-year-old son and two dozen hastily packed cartons, moving on to apartments uptown, to other failed loves, to the loneliness and freedom of a single woman. Once Daniel and I were gone, Peter had thrown out most of the remaining furniture, torn down walls that had temporarily demarcated rooms, demolishing the physical barriers between his life and his painting. Apart from a cot pushed into a corner, old tables splattered with acrylics, growing racks of unsold canvases, his space was finally unobstructed.*

*During the five years of our marriage, he'd never seemed to have room enough. "Tell the child to be quiet," he'd call to me from the studio over the intervening distance of one hundred feet. "Tell him yourself!" I'd yell back. For a while we shared the fantasy that we could achieve harmony by finding an additional place in the country to expand into—a dilapidated farmhouse with a big dairy barn, an abandoned furniture factory near a river. We'd order catalogs from Century 21 and comb them for handyman's specials, constructing some new way of life from the blurry photos of likely prospects. But even the most incredible bargains were beyond the means of a couple without savings.*

*I was fifty by the time I found my own small summer cabin in Vermont. In the years after his friend Maggie Poor died, Peter visited me there several times. By then our estrangement had long since evolved into what I sometimes thought of as cousinship, or at least a genuine but wary affection.*

*He was difficult as a houseguest in some of the ways he'd been difficult as a husband, again seeming to claim all the available space—his socks, his books, his half-unpacked bag on the pine floor of the living room, his shirts and sweaters on the backs of chairs. I'd tactfully point out a chest where he might put things away, and he'd nod his head and ignore the suggestion. But he'd readily volunteer to put shelves up for me, selecting the perfect boards at the lumberyard, taking meticulous measurements, which he'd mark with a carpenter's pencil. This was the proper work for a man, not picking things up. The times had changed, but he had not—at least not in respect to women. It was comical, actually, the way a sixty-year-old man could be as clueless* about certain matters as he'd been in his youth, but in me there'd be the stirrings of old bitter feelings despite the progress I'd made in forgiving him.

My country friends enjoyed Peter's visits and were intrigued by what one of them called our "experiment in living." For two weeks we'd be a couple again, going out to dinner with other middle-aged couples—there always seemed to be many more invitations now that Peter was around, relieving me of the burden of my awkward singleness, evening up the number of seats around a table. Without a word he'd take over the wheel of the Honda, though years after I left him, I had finally learned to drive. Going home along the dirt roads, I'd sit beside him in the dark, drowned in his smoky, salty smell, which seemed to fill the car, chiding him at times for going too fast with so many deer in the woods, sounding for all the world like a real wife, except that once we were in my house, we'd go to our separate rooms, our separate beds, and what we actually were to each other would once again be clear. I'd lie awake propped up on my pillows and hear him cough or turn or shift, and then I'd wait for him to turn off his light. I'd lie awake, wondering if what I felt was the ghost of desire, deciding with relief that wasn't the case. Maybe when we're really old, I'd sometimes think, Peter and I will end up living together, after all.

One Friday night in 1964, I found myself at a party in a crowded East Village walk-up, standing back just as I used to with a glass of wine in my hand. I remember the feeling of having come full circle. It was October, not even a year since I'd waited for Jim in the first December snow as it grew later and later. I wasn't expecting to meet anyone that night, only three weeks after my return to New York, though maybe I hoped to. I know now that I wasn't ready.

I'd fled to Europe in February—stayed away just long enough for people to forget to treat me with extreme care and speak to me in hushed tones. No one knew what to do with a twenty-seven-year-old widow—the widow least of all. The only idea that had occurred to me was to go as far away as I could—as if I were finally embarking on the solitary journey that falling in love with Jim had postponed. I'd found my old job at William Morrow waiting for me when I came back, and I'd just moved into a tiny apartment on the top floor of a brick town house on Jane Street—a neighborhood chosen for its lack of associations. From my bedroom window, I could see a glint of the Hudson.

Perhaps outwardly I seemed my old self again, the self that had pre-dated Jim, as if I had somehow grown younger. After work, I often hung out with an old friend named Connie, whose capacity to be oblivious, brash, and insensitive suddenly seemed a great virtue. It was Connie's ambition to capture an artist husband, preferably thin, blond, blue-eyed, and remote. "Let's go out and meet men," she'd tastelessly propose, and I'd tag along to gallery openings, nights at the Cedar Bar.

Many things had subtly changed during my absence. I noticed that music had entered a new phase—at loft parties Jim and I had danced to Chubby Checker, but Connie informed me he was passé. America was in the grip of Beatlemania; young men were beginning to grow their hair down to their shoulders, like the kids I'd initially stared at in disbelief on the streets of London. People were drinking less, taking more drugs, which made for less conversation in the Cedar. Parties were all about dancing to the point of happy exhaustion, with a minimum of verbal interchange.

Connie and I had been escorted to this one by a middle-aged abstract painter named Julius Tobias, who I feared had designs on me. "I need a woman," he'd proclaim. "Which woman?" I'd ask him. Tobias didn't know the new dance steps and wasn't about to learn them. He positioned himself near the wine table and glowered into the sea of rocking hips as the cracked tenement floorboards shook and vibrated under him. "We might as well leave," he growled. "There's no one here."

At which point a very tall young man politely greeted Tobias and said something about about a show in a co-op gallery on Tenth Street, in which they both had paintings. He had a long bony face with a seriously prominent nose and looked engagingly boyish with his dark blond hair curling upward from his forehead and the tails of his blue work shirt hanging out over his jeans, as if he were still outgrowing his clothes. When Tobias grudgingly introduced him to Connie and me, I was amused by his name, Peter Pinchbeck, which Dickens or Thackeray could have dreamed up. But the slight brogue in Peter's voice seemed more Irish than British.

He turned to me and said casually, "Do you want to dance?" and I found myself saying yes.

He was a rather awkward dancer, and he towered above me, stooping as he shifted his long body from side to side, but he was tireless and enthusiastic and didn't seem to notice when I missed a beat or two myself. We shouted to each other over the music.

"Where are you from, Peter?"

"London."

"I've just come back from there myself."

"So that's why I've never seen you before."

I liked the idea that he'd never seen me and didn't know who I was or what had happened to me. He simply saw a woman he wanted to dance with that particular night, and he didn't seem disposed to stop. When one number ended and another began, we just kept going.

"Are you with Tobias?" he shouted.

"Not really," I shouted back.

"Didn't think you were," he answered with a grin.

When he put me in a cab a couple of hours later, he wrote his address and phone number on a napkin in bold rawboned letters. He had just moved into the first studio he'd ever had in a loft on the Bowery, and he wanted me to stop by there some time so that he could show me some work he'd recently finished and was feeling very excited about. "Just call when you feel like coming over," he said and went back upstairs to the party to do some more dancing.

I'd crossed the Atlantic on a one-way ticket and had come very close to staying abroad. With only a city to return to, why go back? After sitting in cafés in Montparnasse, seeing the Alps and the Duomo and the statue of David, I'd stopped being a tourist and had settled down in London. It wasn't that I was happy there, but I was at home in the language, and I was in my father's country—he had always meant to go back for one more look. Instinctively, without even intending to, I'd begun putting down roots. I watched myself acquire a teapot, then a cup and saucer, a vase, a portable typewriter, an accumulation of books. After some misadventures with nutty landladies in Bloomsbury and South Kensington, I'd moved into a large airy room in Earls Court. It had tall French windows overlooking an unweeded garden and a two-burner stove, where I managed to cook my meals quite successfully with the aid of a paperback on bed-sitter cooking. At Finch's, the nearest bohemian pub on Fulham Road, I'd been taken under the wing of a literary couple who offered to help me get a job in British publishing if I decided I wanted one.

I'd even found a good friend in Hazel Urban, who managed the house in Earls Court and lived in the basement with her seven-year-old daughter. Hazel had recently been deserted by her scoundrel of a husband, a handsome Frenchman who had gambled away all his earnings and hers at dog races; in an advanced stage of pregnancy by the time I met her, she trudged upstairs and down with armloads of linens or the garbage people left outside their doors. But she wasn't the kind of woman who gave in to despair. She derived great comfort and amusement from her knowledge of the macabre side of London, pointing out buildings as we walked around various neighborhoods together where sensational murders had taken place—"Look up there, dear, at the windows on the second floor. That's where fifteen women were given acid baths and no one the wiser."

Hazel claimed to have a special psychic feeling for buildings; she'd been known to turn down perfectly good flats when they were offered to her because "something very odd" had happened there. Odd things had happened in our building in Earls Court, but nothing too bad, maybe just a suicide or two of the garden variety. Bed-sitters, according to Hazel, seemed to lend themselves to suicide—something about the loneliness emitted by the rented furnishings, the temptation of those little gas heaters in the fireplace you could activate with a sixpence. "Sometimes you hear a pop, dear, then breaking glass, and you know another poor soul has done himself in. You'll never do yourself in," she assured me, "and neither will Hazel Urban."

Once I told Hazel that even in London, I was sometimes convinced I saw Jim—a familiar figure just up ahead on a motorcycle with the wind gathering under his jacket or a man with thick wavy brown hair boarding a red double-decker bus. I asked her if she thought that was crazy. "Well, of course you see him," she said. "You'll see him for a while longer, and then you won't."

I saw him, and I also found that he inhabited me. I'd walk into an art gallery on Regent Street, and he'd say from somewhere inside me, "Which one of these paintings do you want me to put my foot through?" Or I'd open my eyes in the morning and hear him murmur, "Scrooch over." But I didn't talk about Jim to most of the people I met. That was the point of being abroad—not having a known history, seeing if I could start over again from scratch. In New York, I'd been afraid of actually turning into the pallid invalid everyone was treating so solicitously. "Either you'll live or you'll die," I kept telling myself—the words were in Jim's voice.

Living, I knew, meant living fully—eventually loving another man, getting married again, having a child. But it was Jim's child I wanted, the one *he* would have given me. For one strange, almost euphoric week in January I'd been convinced I was pregnant—when my period came, I'd wept.

On the huge ocean liner that carried me to Le Havre, I'd precipitously found myself "in love" with another passenger. The affair consumed three days. Since neither he nor I had a private cabin, we resorted to locking ourselves in a shower room to make love on the white-tiled floor in a tangle of flung-down towels; his skin burned against mine as if he had a fever. At Dover, he disembarked, promising to write to me in Paris care of American Express, but when I met him ashore a couple of months later at the British Museum, we had little to say to each other, and after a few more encounters, we parted in mutual embarrassment.

He looked like a weather-beaten cowboy, gaunt and red-haired, but was actually an Englishman, educated at Eton, who had lost his way in America after the war. He had done many things— written songs, been a rodeo rider, worked as a movie stuntman, opened a coffeehouse in Boston. But nothing had panned out, and drink had ruined his health and his marriage. Now a prodigal son of forty, he was returning to live with his elderly parents outside

London because he had nowhere else to go. He'd survived five years at sea on a succession of British destroyers and suspected he'd become permanently unhinged as a result.

I remember the stormy afternoon I first encountered him—I found him out on deck when I ventured up there, hoping to see the phenomenon of white water Jim had often talked about. "Do you think this is white water?" I asked him.

He laughed. "I would say so."

We seemed to be about the only passengers still maintaining upright positions. I clung to a steel cable, and we talked, getting soaked to the skin, until a deckhand insisted we go below. In the deserted second-class cocktail bar, we watched wave after wave lash against the thick glass of the portholes. "If we opened these up—" he suddenly said, "if we opened these up, we could let them in, all my dead friends from the bottom of the sea."

Jim inhabited him, too.


I didn't call Peter Pinchbeck right away. I kept putting it off. I seemed to have lost the courage of someone with nothing to lose that had carried me all through my travels, opened my eyes to possibilities in even the smallest encounters with strangers. In New York, days seemed to pass very slowly. It took all my energy to go back and forth to my job, stepping across the patch of sidewalk on Fourth Avenue where I'd waited for Jim. Upstairs, with a red pencil in my hand, I knew who I was—I was there to make marks on manuscripts, to fix things like a good mechanic. Released to myself at the end of the day, I felt bewildered. In the disquieting twilight, I'd hesitate on the corner of Twenty-ninth Street, wondering whether to walk east or west, uptown or down, as if I were trying to solve a philosphical problem. So much freedom seemed intolerably oppressive.

"Call him," Connie would urge me. "He's the best-looking thing around." I didn't know why this call I wasn't making to Peter Pinchbeck seemed so important to her.

"Call him yourself, then. I'll give you the number."

"I'm not the one he asked."

I wasn't sure I still had the number. But one night I emptied out my handbag, and there at the bottom was the napkin, somewhat the worse for wear.

When I called, I didn't think Peter Pinchbeck remembered who I was. "I'm Tobias's friend—from the party on Avenue B."

"Oh, yes," he said after a slight pause. "The one back from London. How are you?" he said with a surge of enthusiasm.

"Don't ask me that. Disoriented is the word."

"Well, do you feel too disoriented to come by tomorrow afternoon?"

I remember being amused by the elaborate directions he felt it necessary to provide, as if he'd mistaken me for someone who'd led a sheltered life. The building looked unsavory because of the flophouse next door. The entrance was locked, but the buzzer actually worked. He would look out his window on the second floor, then come immediately downstairs. "Just ignore the bums if you can."

"I used to live near the Bowery," I said, and felt the slight shift inside me of things beginning to move back into the past.

There was something about Peter, when I first knew him, that reminded me why I'd decided to come back—an energy, an exuberant optimism, I hadn't found in anyone I'd met abroad. He'd only been in the United States a couple of years, after cooling his heels in Canada until some distant cousins in Connecticut had reluctantly agreed to sponsor his emigration. But his heart had been set upon leaving England ever since his first sight of American abstract painting at an exhibition in London. America was the country where he knew he belonged and to which he swore allegiance—the America, or rather the downtown New York, of de Kooning, Kline, and Pollock, where you needed no credentials to be an artist, where breakthroughs into new territory on or even off the canvas were enough to establish you. His boyish geniality disguised his single-minded determination.

The loft Peter had recently moved into, less than half the size of the one where I'd lived with Jim, was already looking too small for him. Two old library tables someone had given him—covered with drawings, sawdust, coffee mugs, tubes of paint squeezed almost flat—occupied the center of the space. Paintings had been pushed out of the way of boxy forms of various sizes that were being made out of plywood for some mysterious purpose. Peter was still nailing metal plates over holes in the floorboards, but had otherwise left the loft much as he'd found it in his impatience to get to work. The walls had not been plastered or whitened in twenty years. You had to look around to find the bed—a couple of Salvation Army mattresses covered by an army blanket, set on bricks stolen from a construction site. He was as proud of the place as if it were beautiful. He went to a rusting industrial sink, rinsed out a coffee mug, and offered me some wine.

I'd instinctively understood Jim's paintings at first sight; but I still remember how the almost defiant awkwardness of the ones Peter showed me took me aback. Why were those flat squares superimposed on abstract expressionist backgrounds? Why were the colors so weird? Yet I sensed you had to respect all that newness that delivered such a shock to the eyes.

I doubt those paintings would seem as alien if I could look at them now. But they weren't long for this world. Peter soon moved on to a minimalist phase and covered them with gesso so that he could reuse the canvas. All through his career, circumstances would force him to eradicate his footsteps. At the very beginning, though, he expressed little regret. He was working fast and hungrily, absorbing different ideas that were in the air, trying out his take on them. Even during my first visit, he showed me sketches for constructions that would project outward from the wall. That's what those plywood boxes were for.

What did we say to each other as we drank wine from his chipped mugs, sitting side by side on the edge of Peter's mattress due to the absence of chairs? There must have been an uncertain space between us, then something happened or was said that caused him to reach for me with his long arms and push me gently down on the blanket. And I saw him the following day and the next, and quickly it became a fact that Peter was going to be in my life.

"What was I like at that time?" I recently asked an old friend.

She thought a moment and said, "You seemed to be sleepwalking."

Sometimes I asked myself questions about the uncomfortable symmetry of Peter and Jim both being painters, but apart from that, I never felt that Jim inhabited Peter. Surely this was a sign that I had begun to recover, although Jim still inhabited me. It seemed healthy, in fact, that Peter showed little curiosity about him, no curiosity at all really, though he'd listen silently whenever I couldn't stop myself from talking about Jim, which I tried to do less and less.

I soon noticed that the past, including his own, did not seem of much interest to Peter. It was as if he had sternly decided to make no room for it in his thoughts—perhaps that was even one source of his energy. He had left behind a mother in Brighton who had cancer—he couldn't visit her, he said, without losing his green card. I was never shown a picture of Peter's mother, even after she died. He also had a father, alive and well as far as he knew, with whom he'd had no contact for most of his life. The mother was Irish Catholic, and working-class. The father was a direct descendant of the eighteenth-century alchemist Christopher Pinchbeck, notorious in his day for making false gold that looked like the real thing. There was even a village somewhere in England called East Pinchbeck—it surprised me that Peter had never thought of visiting it. The British class system, Peter explained, had caused his father to desert his mother soon after his birth. He had a funny way of referring to his native land—it was "*that* country," as if he'd never had a connection to it. My own affection for England, he assured me, was only the misguided partiality of a tourist.

During his brief time in the British Army, Peter had narrowly escaped an ironic fate. Because he was a six-footer, they'd wanted to post him to serve as a guard at Buckingham Palace. Fortunately,

his slouching posture had saved him from the indignity of having to march up and down in the service of the queen, wearing one of those ridiculous red uniforms and bearskin hats.

He was sure he would have been even taller if the war hadn't started when he was eight. Throughout much of the Blitz Peter and his mother had been on their own in London, and there often hadn't been much to eat. My efforts to get him to talk about the war were never very successful. He alluded a few times to being bombed out and having to live in an old trailer until his mother found a job keeping house for a priest. That was the low point, being in that house, but he never said why, though he had no use for the Catholic Church. There was something else I always wondered about—something about seeing a baby with a head injury after an air raid, blood covering its skull. After that he'd become sort of horrified by babies, their baldness, their helplessness; he didn't mind them so much if they had hair.

We went dancing a lot—I seem to remember that it was almost every night. An enormous bar where you could dance, called the Dom, had opened in a cellar on St. Marks Place, and soon there was a similar joint on Avenue A. Our dancing didn't improve, but it was awfully energetic. A faceted glass ball revolved from the ceiling, half blinding you as you moved and shook in time with the rest of the crowd, and the throbbing music got inside your head, crowding out any thoughts that were too complicated or dark.

It was easy to be with Peter, it was fun. I'd never been with anyone who seemed to have so little in the way of "baggage." But one night, after we'd been going out for a few weeks, the buzzer unexpectedly sounded in his loft while I was visiting him there. His face stiffened—his expression became unusually grim; he didn't walk to the window or take a look downstairs. "It must be one of the bums," Peter said. But whoever it was kept repeatedly pressing the buzzer before giving up and going away.

He'd invited me to the opening of a group show on Tenth Street that weekend, where he'd installed a couple of his latest paintings; afterward friends were supposed to bring wine over to his loft for a party. A day before the opening, he called and asked me not to come, sounding very embarrassed. There was something he should have told me about, but he hadn't, hoping it would just blow over. He'd mistakenly gotten himself involved with someone over the summer, a married woman who wouldn't leave him alone and was probably mentally unbalanced. He'd heard she planned to show up at the gallery and was afraid she'd make a scene if she found him with anyone else. He thought it best to humor her at present—he didn't know what else to do. He'd deal with her, then we'd see each other.

I wondered if he'd be back. I had often observed that unbalanced women were likely to succeed in holding on to their men, especially men as good-hearted and innocent as Peter. Experience had made me quite cynical, I thought, compared to him.

As a week passed, I found myself missing Peter acutely, more than I'd even expected to. We'd simply fallen in with each other—I hadn't thought very much before about what it meant. When he finally reappeared, turning up at my apartment on Jane Street one night after I'd gone to bed, I was too relieved to ask him whether the unbalanced woman was really out of his life. I made room for him under the covers, and he whispered something—"Wait for me"—and I said I would.

I'm struck by how poorly I remember this whole period—as if I were floating through it, never giving it my entire attention. I can't remember either of us ever saying, "I love you." We probably did, but I'm not absolutely sure. No one could ever get truly close to Peter, not all the way—maybe we picked each other for that reason.

When I'd moved everything out of Chrystie Street just before I fled to Europe, I'd stored Jim's paintings in another loft on the Bowery. I was afraid to go over there and look at them, but finally I did one Sunday afternoon in November. Dominick Capobianco, the artist who'd rented me the space, had barely known Jim, but he'd come to think a great deal of the paintings. Patiently pulling them out for me one by one, he propped them against walls until they surrounded me. Seeing them again, I almost fainted. For me there was more than oil and acrylics on those canvases; there was blood and bone and breath. Twenty-two months . . . I saw our lives painted there.

"You should do something with these," Dominick said.

For months I'd been thinking about what could be done, what I could manage to do alone, since there was no one else to do anything for Jim's work. I often wondered whether there would continue to be art if artists ever lost their mad belief in posterity. I'd had it too when I was writing my first novel, then lost it when it became clear that few people would ever read it. But Jim's conviction that what he was creating would eventually find its place in the world had remained unshaken. I had to find a way of proving that he was right.

I learned that the art dealer who had given Jim his last two shows in Cleveland was about to open a gallery in New York on Fifty-seventh Street. How could he refuse to at least look at Jim's paintings?

After several fruitless phone calls, I managed to get a five-minute appointment with this man in his elegant office, adjoining a vast empty space still under construction. Of course he remembered Jim, he told me, remembered him fondly, but no, he couldn't help. There was no market whatsoever for second-generation abstract expressionism by a complete unknown. He intended to devote his gallery to op art, geometric abstraction, minimalism; if Jim had lived and still hoped to sell, he would have had to move on into one of these exciting new areas, which might have been difficult for him, considering his temperament. The dealer shook my hand and asked his secretary to send in his next appointment.

I knew this was the way the art world worked, but I took it hard. "It's capitalism," Peter said. "What did you expect?" Finally I decided the only thing I could possibly do on my limited resources was arrange to have a memorial show at St. Mark's-in-the-Bouwerie, an East Village church that had become a gathering place for poets and artists. Peter bowled me over by immediately offering to do most of the work. He would move everything in a rented truck and hang the show himself; he had an idea for the flyer, which he thought should be very stark—was there a black-and-white drawing that we could use?

To make the first rough selection of what should be hung, he went with me to Dominick's. Narrowing his gray eyes, he considered each painting thoughtfully, stepping back and forth till he stood at the proper distance. He didn't tell me what he thought of Jim's work, and I wondered if it was uncomfortable for Peter to actually confront it, if he couldn't help asking himself how his own work stood up to Jim's. But he said there was no question it should be shown.

The show went up in St. Mark's parish hall in January. I remember we found the walls dismayingly grimy and spent much of the day before the opening scrubbing them. Still, the paintings looked beautiful—everyone said so. The crowd at the opening filled the hall and consumed all the wine we'd put out.

At the last moment, Peter had reminded me to assign a price to each of the canvases. I'd felt terribly reluctant to do so. Prices? I didn't want to part with any of them through meaningless transactions—I just wanted them to hang in that big white room until thousands of people had seen them and they were placed in museums where they belonged. I waited for some sign that Jim would have his shot at posterity. But except for one review in the *Village Voice,* nothing happened, not one sale—nothing opening up into the future. After three weeks the show came down and went back into storage. I took a few of the smallest paintings—including two Jim had painted on the mailbag—home to my tiny apartment.

I left Jane Street in the spring and moved east to my old neighborhood into a much larger and nicer apartment on St. Marks Place. It was on the parlor floor, and its high ceiling and two tall front windows reminded me of my bed-sitter in Earls Court. St. Marks Place had become the busiest thoroughfare of the East Village. As the weather got warmer, I often stood at one of the windows to watch the tumultuous street life roll by, whiffs of marijuana from musicians strolling to their gigs in the jazz club on the corner rising to my nostrils.

I'd moved, aside from other excellent reasons, to be closer to Peter, for Peter to be closer to me. It didn't take long at all for him to walk from the Bowery to my new address. Soon we were spending all our nights together. He brought in a toothbrush; his tattered socks and faded blue work shirts got mixed into the bag I dropped off at the laundromat. Our dancing continued unabated, preceded now by the meals I began making for both of us.

Peter was enthusiastic about my cooking, which included some green vegetables that at first he regarded dubiously. Left to his own devices, he lived uncomplainingly on Mrs. Wagner's frozen fish sticks, Campbell's soup, Heinz baked beans. He knew how to make instant coffee and heat things on a hot plate but had no interest in learning what went on in an actual kitchen. "You're hopeless!" I'd tell him.

I learned that right after Peter had been let into America, he'd had to take a menial job in the depths of the Union Square subway station. All day long, in a white coverall and a ridiculous matching soldier's cap, he'd halved oranges to feed into the funnel of a very poorly designed juicing device that once went absolutely haywire, erupting sticky fluid all over him and the enraged customers at the stand, resulting in his getting fired. Peter implied that this trauma had somehow confirmed him in his hopelessness. But his proud undomesticatability seemed part of his charm.

I listened with poker-faced indulgence whenever Peter inveighed—*inveighed* was the word—against the institutions of marriage and parenthood, both of which he had ruled out for himself. Artists had no business being married, bourgeois comfort was a trap, children were a luxury he could neither afford nor support—not that he had anything against them, but he had to put all his attention elsewhere. Let the bourgeoisie have babies and raise them in Westchester County! Carried away to indignant Shavian heights like the soapbox orators I'd heard on Hyde Park Corner, he seemed to forget completely that I was his girlfriend, rather than a fellow iconoclast who shared his antipathy toward the whole idea of the nuclear family.

I didn't reason with him, I just listened to him rage on; sometimes it was hard not to laugh. How young Peter sounded, I thought, with all his abstract ideas, his certainties. How amazingly little he knew about real life, despite the hard times he'd had growing up in England. But now I think he knew a great deal about himself, about his own limits, though some of his fervor that spring can be attributed to the fact that the unbalanced woman had just given birth to a boy she claimed was his.

Peter was certain—or at least convinced himself and me, because I wanted to be convinced—that he couldn't possibly be the father. The woman not only had a husband but had carried on the previous summer, when Peter had met her on Cape Cod, with various other men. Unfortunately, Peter was the one she was determined to end up with. It was clear she'd hoped the pregnancy would ensnare him.

A disgusting reason, I thought, to have a child! You should only want a child for itself, and if you didn't really want it, you shouldn't bring it into the world. I'd been on my own since I was nineteen, and every now and then I realized how it had hardened me—I didn't have much sympathy for a woman of thirty-five who wouldn't take care of herself.

The woman had kept calling Peter, sending him threatening notes, cloying love letters, ringing his doorbell. She called him from the hospital, demanded he come and see the baby when her husband wasn't around. Looking ashen, he asked me if he had to go. I told him he didn't, but sometimes I felt a little guilty when I thought about the kid. Sometimes I still wonder if it looked like Peter. But I think he always ruled out the possibility.

On my two-week vacation in August, we went away to Provincetown. Peter had been very taken with the place the previous year, especially with the quality of the light. I doubt he ever went anywhere without wondering whether it would be a good place to make art. He had stern things to say about the corny representational seascapes hanging in Provincetown restaurants and took down a still life in the room where we were staying and put it in a drawer. I teased him about the way he even looked at sunsets with a critical eye as we stood at the end of the town pier, watching the sky put on its nightly show, but I always felt sad out there, watching the fishing boats come in, the gulls wheeling overhead—I couldn't help missing Jim.

One night in a bar where we went dancing, Peter got into a fight because a man at the next table had started coming on to me the moment Peter went to get beer and was still insisting that I dance with him when Peter returned. I have a distinct recollection of Peter saying, "Lay off her, buddy," with his slight brogue and of tables and chairs suddenly flying in every direction, as I looked on in amazement. This was a side of Peter I'd never seen. I realized he'd come to think of me as his.

I remember the first sign I was pregnant—a weirdly intense hunger that overwhelmed me one day between floors in Altman's department store. I was going up on a very slow escalator, and all at once I knew I'd better find a place to sit down, because I'd never felt so ravenous in my life. The feeling passed, but it stayed on my mind. A week went by. It was the middle of October. I'd been expecting to get my period, but it never came. Without saying anything to Peter, I had myself tested and learned I was going to have a baby.

I couldn't believe it at first—I'd never made love with Peter without using a birth control device. But it was true, dazzlingly true once the fact had sunk in, sweeping all practical considerations aside. Never mind that I wasn't married, that the timing was awful, the conditions totally uncertain—there would be this child, and somehow I'd manage. Something told me I'd never have another chance.

Of course this was nothing Peter had bargained for. I remember feeling sorry for him in a protective way, hugely embarrassed, as if I were reneging on a deal. The unbalanced woman was still pursuing him with raging letters. Once I'd walked past her on St. Marks Place wheeling her carriage, and she'd grabbed at my arm, shrieking, "Look what you've done!" and tried to push me to the ground. I was sure she'd regard my pregnancy, if she heard about it, as divine retribution. Undoubtedly, Peter would see it as a disaster that had overtaken him of almost comically ludicrous proportions.

It took me a few days before I found the courage to break the news after he'd innocently walked in one evening, expecting nothing more momentous than dinner. I put two plates on the round oak table that had been present during so much of my history and poured him a glass of wine. "We're having a baby, Peter," I said.

He put down the glass, an uncertain smile on his face, as if he were waiting for the rest of this not very funny joke.

"If you want to stick around and be part of this, that would be terrific," I plunged on. "If you don't, I'll understand. But I'll have the baby anyway, and I won't ask you for anything." All these words had been revised and rehearsed endlessly in my mind.

I remember a very long silence. And then Peter said in a stunned voice, "I think we'd better get married pretty soon."

It was a response that went against all his principles, against anything I had truly expected of him. So I promised Peter his life wouldn't change—I'd see to that.

We got married in City Hall about two weeks later, standing in line for our turn with the justice of the peace, celebrating with lunch in Chinatown. This time I didn't feel much like a bride. I'd told my mother and everyone at work that Peter and I had married secretly in Provincetown that summer, and I wondered if anyone believed me, though no one asked me why it had to be a secret.

My mother didn't take well to the news—"*Another* Greenwich Village marriage!"

On my lunch hours, I started going to thrift shops to hunt for baby clothes. There wasn't going to be much money to live on once I started paying for a sitter. Sometimes I felt almost dizzy wondering how I'd handle all the arrangements for the baby. I thought about everything I'd have to do, as if Peter wouldn't be there. I was grateful that whatever he was thinking, he no longer made diatribes against the nuclear family.

His mind was on his work. The imminent arrival of the baby didn't seem very real to him once the shock of first hearing about it had passed. I had dreams about crying infants—sometimes I knew the babies were Jim's. I wondered if Peter's dreams were filled with tall wooden boxes, painted in bright colors, standing in groups at odd angles in the midst of vast empty lofts. He had become more and more obsessed with geometry, with an aesthetic of straight lines. He talked excitedly of Albers, Malevich, the Russian Constructivists, of the way three-dimensional objects defined the space around them. It was painful for him to wrench himself away from the studio to do the carpentry, house-painting, and proofreading jobs that provided him with money for rent and materials and his cans of beans. Other artists had begun making geometric constructions out of steel, but Peter could only afford plywood. That limitation also became part of his aesthetic—a geometry with soft edges where you could still see the artist's hand, brush strokes rather than a smooth machine-made finish, faint pockmarks under the coats of paint where nails had been driven in.

In May there was going to be an important exhibition at the Jewish Museum. It would be called *Primary Structures* and would feature the latest work in geometric abstraction by a whole crop of new artists. When Peter was invited to have a piece in it, there was no doubt in his mind that he was finally on his way—soon he'd have a gallery, he told me, a one-man show, maybe even a bank account. From one work in the Jewish Museum an entire career would flow.

All spring he worked on his piece, the most difficult construction he'd ever attempted: two tall, perfectly proportioned rectangular boxes of identical height and width. One of them had a concave side—a generous arc curving inward, like a reverse pregnancy, I realize now. Peter painted them red, coat upon coat, and positioned them side by side with a slight but distinct separation between them that made the arc he had cut out all the more compelling. One night he called me from the studio and said the piece was done and asked me to come over and see it. I stared at it a long

time. Those two red forms had a deceptive simplicity, an absolute
purity. They moved me, and I didn't know why. Once again Peter
had taken me by surprise.

I went to the opening hugely pregnant in a green-and-white
tent dress I had made for the occasion. Peter's piece, I noted, had a
human warmth missing in most of the other work. It was a stand-
out, I thought proudly, not considering the possible consequences
of standing too much apart as a maverick in this new movement
of minimalist art. He was buoyant that night, radiantly confident.
It was the last time his work was ever shown in a major museum
show in New York.

Our baby arrived two weeks before we'd expected him, on June
15, not long after the opening at the Jewish Museum. Somehow
I'd never doubted I'd have a boy. His name was waiting for him—
Daniel, after my father. I'd worried a little—because of Peter's
odd squeamishness about babies' naked, vulnerable heads—that
he wouldn't have hair. Fortunately, he did—a shock of red that
stood straight up and soon turned blond. Peter consented to hold
him against his shoulder during visiting hours, but after a minute
or two he'd say hastily, "You'd better take the little fallow." I was
terrified myself as well as thrilled—when it came to handling an
infant, I was a complete amateur. Cold sweat ran down my back
the first time I tried to put an undershirt on the baby—I hoped he
would forgive the ineptitude of his mother.

We brought Daniel home to St. Marks Place in a taxi that got
stuck in heavy traffic on the East River Drive—heat poured in
through the open windows, gas fumes filled the air, sirens
screeched by. Peter and I turned to each other with the same
thought—this was a hell of a way to welcome a brand-new human
being to the world.

* * *

The following couple of years lack definition for me now—they're a smogged-over terrain, where I can barely make out the blurred figure of a woman. The woman is running, running in circles—from the baby to the subway, from the subway to the job, from the

job to the subway, to the supermarket, to the apartment, which is never clean enough, where the sitter is waiting to immediately hand over the baby, who needs to be played with, who needs a clean diaper and a bath before the husband comes home needing dinner, which there really isn't time to make but somehow gets made anyway, leaving a sinkful of dirty pots and dishes which will have to be washed once the baby is put to bed, by which time the husband has gone out for the evening and the woman is free to amuse herself as the laundry churns in the washing machine or to black out until the reentry of the husband, the two A.M. feeding, the four A.M. diaper change, the bleary beginning of a new day.

I didn't question these arrangements—it would have taken

more energy than I could afford, though at first I kept hoping Peter would notice I needed a little help. It was true I'd made a bargain with him. But I'd never imagined how hard it would be or that his part of it would be sustained to the letter. Besides, although unlike most new mothers I had to earn a living, the division—or rather, lack of division—of labor in our household was certainly traditional. Peter's life, as I'd promised him, had hardly changed at all, apart from the beguiling, sometimes noisy presence of the baby or the fact that once I was home from the office and the baby-sitter had gone, I could no longer go out with my former dancing companion—or go anywhere on impulse, perhaps for the rest of my life.

Peter admired the baby greatly—from a distance, as if it were a small work of art you had to stand back from to properly appreciate. I kept waiting for him to turn into a father, but he remained a baby admirer, a sort of detached bachelor uncle, intrigued but wary of involvement. Perhaps a man who'd had no paternal models to go by could not become a father overnight—perhaps it would take a great deal of time. But I couldn't help comparing Peter to Jim, remembering Jim's passionate feelings for the kids he'd lost. I was sure Jim would have immediately given up the motorcycle if I'd gotten pregnant. But would he have stopped drinking for good? I wondered. Would I ever have had to take another child away from him? What could you make of a story that wouldn't let you go because it had never been fully worked out?

And where was I now? I began asking that question too. How had I misplaced the woman Jim had glimpsed behind the one who stood back, the woman who'd gone into permanent retreat after he died?

We weren't living far from my old East Village apartment. I often went out to First Avenue with the baby to buy vegetables, but there was never any reason for me to shop below St. Marks Place. One day, though, in early spring, I wheeled the baby carriage a bit farther downtown. Tucked under his plaid blanket, one fist against his round, moist cheek, my son was sleeping beatifically—whenever I glanced down at him, I somehow felt a little protected from the past, safe enough to walk to Fifth Street.

I resolutely crossed First Avenue to get a good look at the second floor of the brick building where Jim and I had started out. The two front windows I'd always kept bare were covered now by net curtains, but on the fire escape I saw an empty flowerpot I was sure I'd left behind when we moved to Chrystie Street. Suddenly my former landlord emerged from his linoleum store and walked up the block.

I'd often stared across First Avenue to exactly where I was now standing. It was strange to think I'd become part of the view. Traffic went by, as it always had. The baby yawned in the carriage, then went back to sleep. I waited for someone to come to the window, pull aside a curtain, but no one did.

In what is now called SoHo, there's a loft building on Greene Street, so altered with its freshly painted cream-colored facade and the street-level boutique selling improbable French designer clothes that I scarcely recognize it when I happen to pass by, although I lived there with Peter for the last two years of our marriage. I'd bump Daniel's stroller up the two steps of the metal loading platform that no longer exists and struggle into the freight elevator, standing on tiptoe to pull at the heavy steel door that slammed down alarmingly from the top. I'd never encountered an elevator that reminded me of a guillotine, but eventually I got used to it and felt rather proud of my prowess—until I got unused to it all over again after my departure. As the decades rolled by and Greene Street began reinventing itself with higher and higher real estate values, I came to think of that elevator as the entrance to Peter's fortress—like a moat, it seemed to protect him from the inroads of gentrification, from the changing trends in the art world.

When the three of us moved to Greene Street in the summer of '69, I think Peter and I both had hopes that this new experiment in living would hold us together. Something was clearly going wrong with our marriage, though neither of us would admit it was growing cold. For a while Peter had been saying he thought he'd be much happier if everything could be brought together under one roof—if he didn't have to break into his concentration in the studio to walk over to St. Marks Place. The walk had begun to frustrate him, he said; the artificial separation between life and work could not be good for an artist. I wasn't so sure—I wondered if it would be difficult raising a child inside the place where Peter worked, though I could see the benefits of having Peter right there if I needed him, and I'd been troubled by the frustration he'd sometimes brought home to the apartment. Then Andy Warhol took over Peter's entire building on the Bowery, and that settled the matter.

The SoHo we moved to was an industrial ghost town. Signs hung from every building, advertising the huge empty lofts small factories had given up. For space-hungry painters the area below Houston Street, once called Hell's Hundred Acres, became the new rugged frontier of the New York art world. You did not see movie stars or investment bankers on the bumpy cobblestoned streets, or young women with baby carriages. In the daytime you saw trucks, workmen, heavy machinery, bales of rags bound for papermills—the last gasps of the garment industry. At nighttime you saw no one passing through the dark, silent neighborhood, unless it was an artist you personally knew, a homesteader like yourself, some painter who hadn't made it yet, because those who had, still lived uptown in the midst of civilization. I remember my three dingy summers in SoHo, the absence of color in the streets before the incursion of boutiques, the gray flaking off the old buildings, sifting down to the cobblestones, beams of sunlight swarming with dust. You had to cross Houston Street before you saw a tree.

Peter was in love with the new loft. He would have liked to

leave it just the way he first saw it—2,500 square feet of unobstructed space—but a living area had to be closed off. Our existence as a family required a bathroom large enough for a tub, a place to cook, enough space for our bed and my round table, a room set aside for our son. Reluctantly, Peter erected Sheetrock

walls that stopped short of the ceiling so that heat and air could pass through. Then, with more enthusiasm, he made us a minimalist coffee table—a square white wooden box with cleverly concealed wheels—and turned some plastic tubing into a floor lamp. Before we left St. Marks Place, he'd made me discard a good deal of furniture.

I didn't ask Peter to build me a small office. It would only have reminded me of the novel about Jim I'd started in London, and had put away once I came back. Soon it would be seven years since

I'd published my first novel. Sometimes I wondered if I'd only be able to write again if I lived alone. But the idea of solitude, the peculiar solitude of a woman alone with a child, daunted me, even though there were moments when I allowed myself to imagine what it would be like.

Apart from Peter's excitement about the new loft and his plans to build much larger pieces there, he often seemed glum. There had been no results from the show at the Jewish Museum, and all his efforts to find a gallery kept coming to nothing. He detested the whole process of trying to find a dealer, the humiliation of making the rounds with slides, setting up appointments for studio visits that always seemed to get canceled or postponed, being charming when it didn't suit him to people whose taste he didn't really respect. He couldn't play the game—not even as well as Jim could, because something about Jim's outrageousness had actually attracted collectors, aroused the desire to acquire a piece of the artist. Peter's kind of eccentricity—the dogged seriousness he could never disguise, the anger that began to mount in him noticeably after continual disappointments—did not serve him well as the art world became increasingly giddy and hedonistic. He adhered to the strangely pure idea that the power of his work should speak for itself—with huge fluctuations of hope and despair, he would spend the rest of his life awaiting discovery.

I felt terrible for Peter when I came home one night and found that the red piece from the *Primary Structures* show was gone. Since no one was interested in it, he said, he had put it out on the street that day with the garbage; looking out the front window, he had watched it being loaded into a truck.

* * *

Since we were very broke after the move, one day I asked Peter if there would be room in his studio to store Jim's paintings. He was silent; then he looked away from me and said, "I really don't want them in my space," and I realized I shouldn't have brought up the subject. Instead we moved them into the basement of a building on Canal Street that some painters who were friends of Peter's had just bought. All the painters in the building kept their work down there too; it was supposed to be perfectly safe, and it wouldn't cost us a cent. Until 1971, no one gave any thought to the fact that deep underneath Canal Street were the remains of an old canal. In one week that spring, an unusual amount of rain fell on New York, and without warning, the black waters of the old canal backed up and flooded all the basements. Except for the few small works I'd brought home with me after Jim's show, every stroke Jim had painted in his two last years—every vestige of his fierce final reach for posterity—was wiped out. Lost like my grandfather's poems, as if it were only a myth that art is durable.

A flood like that was a complete fluke, everyone said. There wouldn't be another like it for a century.

In the late 1980s I visited Jim's first wife, who by then had moved from Painesville to a house in Cleveland. All the work he'd done before I met him was stored there, and I was finally able to see the series of red, white, and black canvases that had led to the ones that had been destroyed. Jim's wife had never remarried—she said no one had ever measured up to Jim. I was amazed by her kindness when she offered to give me any painting I wanted.

As Peter's work proliferated and remained unsold, I'd become the breadwinner for all three of us. Fortunately, in our last months on St. Marks Place, I'd found a new and more lucrative job at the Dial Press. I was now earning $7,500 a year rather than $5,000, which immediately made an enormous difference. While I was still at William Morrow, the *New York Times Magazine* had published an article defining the "poverty level"—I'd done some fast arithmetic, subtracting what I was paying the baby-sitter from my salary, and discovered that the poverty level was where we were actually living. I was grateful that Morrow had finally promoted me to editor after I'd worked there seven years, but I was tired of eating chili three times a week and never being able to afford more than one pair of shoes at a time. My indignation prompted me to go after the opening I'd just heard about at the Dial Press.

The editor-in-chief was E. L. Doctorow, who had not yet become famous as a novelist and was trying to write *The Book of Daniel* in whatever time he could wrench from his job. Ed saw the advantages of hiring an editor who could relieve him of doing rewrites and immediately turned over to me his more problematic manuscripts. He also encouraged me to go out and acquire just the kinds of books I'd become most interested in publishing.

In the 1950s, when I'd first read Kerouac, I felt I'd discovered someone who would understand exactly why I'd had to leave home. I was drawn to the Beats because they refused to settle for lives of "quiet desperation," because they challenged the suffocating terms of what constituted respectability. In the New Left rebels and activists of the late 1960s, I found some of the same life-changing energy. Unlike the hippies, they had goals that extended beyond self-transformation. They were out to stop the Vietnam War, to win black people full equality, to change the status of women. I wanted to be part of this movement, but I was a woman who could never get out of the house unless I was on my way to the office, who spent lunch hours searching midtown drugstores for the "revolutionary" disposable diapers that had just appeared on the market. How could I leave Daniel to march in Selma, Alabama, or demonstrate in front of the Pentagon? So books became my contribution. At Morrow, I'd bought books by black intellectuals like LeRoi Jones and Harold Cruse; at Dial, I edited Anne Moody, Julius Lester, and Abbie Hoffman, the brilliant, flamboyant founder of the Yippies, who had a natural instinct for street theater.

Abbie had been my neighbor on St. Marks Place. In the spring of '68, I'd signed him up for an exchange of letters with a more scholarly radical named Daniel Schecter, who was studying at the London School of Economics. This was an idea Abbie would soon cast aside. That summer brought the huge demonstrations against the Vietnam War at the Democratic National Convention in Chicago, where Abbie, one of the leaders, was arrested with hundreds of others, including my old friend Allen Ginsberg.

A few days afterward, I heard my name shouted under the front windows—"Joyce! Joyce! I've got the book!"—and buzzed Abbie in. Daniel was in his high chair eating a banana. Abbie took it and broke it in two. Handing one half back to Daniel, he popped the other in his own mouth as my son stared at him in solemn amazement, not knowing what to make of such a transgression by a grown-up. Abbie informed me that the new book was going to be about Chicago, and that we had to get it out in three weeks. Although the manuscript didn't yet exist, it already had a title: *Revolution for the Hell of It.* We spent the next three weeks sitting on the floor of my office, piecing it together out of scraps of Abbie's writings. When it came out, it quickly sold 100,000 copies. Dial gave me a raise without my even asking for it.

As I went on publishing rebels who wanted to turn the prevailing order upside down, I found it harder and harder to tolerate the constriction, the creeping dreariness, of my own situation. At five P.M., when I was about to leave Dial, where interesting and exciting things seemed to be happening all the time and I was right in the middle of the action, I often felt reluctant to go home, knowing that once I walked in with my sack of manuscripts in one hand, my shopping bag of groceries in the other, I would start to feel diminished, weary, deflated. I would eat dinner with my husband and wonder why I felt I had no one to talk to. It was as if Peter and I were standing at opposite ends of a stage, delivering monologues that never intersected.

If I talked about my latest adventure at Dial or spoke too enthusiastically about a new manuscript, his face would get stony. He had no successes to report. No one was buying Peter's work, and nothing I could say or do seemed to comfort him. I willingly wrote checks when he needed new materials—but that probably only made him feel worse. Perhaps it would have been easier for Peter if I'd hated my job.

Words would come out of his mouth that I found wounding. One night, after mentioning running into an artist we both knew, Peter remarked, apropos of nothing, "Frank is very lucky. He has a beautiful wife."

A hundred caustic rejoinders rose into my throat, but I finished my dinner in silence and was still swallowing my anger as I put the dishes in the sink. I had never quite shaken off my mother's training—another year would pass before I raised my voice.

Meanwhile, Peter's constant presence on the other side of the Sheetrock wall in our new loft made me more and more aware of his maddening remoteness from me and our son. Now that Daniel was older, Peter might consent to watch him on a Saturday afternoon so that I could go to the supermarket, but if Daniel was sick or the baby-sitter didn't show up, that was my problem, not Peter's, even if it meant I had to stay home from the office, because Peter's work could not be interrupted. If he'd offered me any substantial amount of help in return for the help I gave him, then he would have had to acknowledge his humiliating dependency upon a woman.

Still, Daniel made it his business to see more of his father, gravitating toward the sounds of hammering and sawing on the other side of the wall. *Door* had been one of his first words, and he knew how to open the one that led to the studio and ride his tricycle in. Sometimes Peter would give him pieces of wood to play with; then, after a few too many questions from his child, the endless *why*'s of a three-year-old, he'd firmly usher him out, stooping a little to catch hold of his hand. I remember that stoop of Peter's, the suppressed tenderness of it, like the look on his face sometimes

when he held Daniel on his lap. "I don't know anything about little kids," he'd say. "I don't have much feeling for relating to them,
to tell you the truth."

During my second summer on Greene Street, *Newsweek* decided
to run a story about the new wave of best-selling radical books. I
was one of the four editors they'd decided to interview. I had to
stay home from work one morning so that a photographer could
come to the loft to take my picture. Daniel was at nursery school,
and Peter had found an excuse to go out before the photographer
arrived with his lights and white umbrella. When the photo session
finally ended, I found that I had a couple of free hours before I
was expected at Dial. The little gift of unencumbered time felt
very luxurious, and not knowing what else to do with it, I decided
to go in search of Peter, whom I suspected I would find at
Fanelli's, the only bar in the neighborhood. I thought it would be
sort of festive to have lunch with him there.

Peter wasn't alone that day. He was sitting with a painter named
George, with whom he'd been spending a lot of his evenings in
the artists' bars uptown, and a thin young woman with very short
hair, very tight jeans, and a very tight face, whom he introduced to
me as Dawn. Lately I'd been hearing a little too much about
Dawn, whom Peter considered a fascinating new kind of woman.
He didn't know how talented she was, but her avant-garde behavior had impressed him. Dawn had left her two small children in
Michigan with her mother and come to New York to paint. Peter
and I had disagreed as to whether her abandonment of her children constituted gutsiness or lack of maternal feeling.

Dawn cut hair for a living, and as I sat there with the three of
them, she invited Peter and George to come to her loft so that she
could give them haircuts gratis, though she did not extend me a

similar offer. In fact she barely looked in my direction, making it clear she had written me off as a nonperson—a mere wife and mother.

"I'm the only one at this table whose photo is going to appear in *Newsweek,*" I suddenly thought to myself. It was an insight that exploded inside my brain like one of those lightbulb epiphanies in a comic strip. How was it that I could be important enough to have my name in *Newsweek,* while at home I was little more than a housemaid? It didn't add up at all, I realized, and I was going to do something about it, though I wasn't sure what.

By the time I came home from work that evening, I'd figured out what to ask for. "You go out anytime you like," I said to Peter. "I, too, need to go out. We're going to hire a live-in sitter."

Peter looked at me in disbelief. Where would we put such a person? he wanted to know.

"In your studio," I told him. "You have space enough there to build a room."

He didn't argue. I think he knew—even from my tone of voice—that something inside me had changed.

The new sitter, a disoriented French student who had just landed in the States and knew little English, moved in a couple of weeks later. Peter found himself another small loft in the neighborhood—a place to retreat to, he said, when he needed to concentrate, especially on weekends when Daniel was around all day and I was home from the office.

I wonder what the French sitter made of our typical American household, because in the middle of her first night, just a few hours after she'd unpacked and gone to bed, the lights went on in the studio and there was a lot of angry shouting, and after that, Peter disappeared.

I had tried out my brand-new freedom, after I'd put Daniel to bed, by calling George's wife, Rosemary, announcing that I had a sitter, and suggesting that she and I go out together. "Let's walk up to Remington's," she said, "and surprise the boys." Remington's, a new bar in Greenwich Village, was the latest artists' hangout, and George and Peter were going there nightly. In fact, lately it had become so hard for Peter to tear himself away that he seldom came home before four in the morning. I had never seen the place and was curious about its attractions. When I walked in with Rosemary and looked around, my eyes fell upon Peter sitting in a booth with a young woman. He saw me and froze, then went back to his conversation with her as if I weren't there.

"Be cool," Rosemary murmured to me. And for a while I was. I sat at the bar with her and had a drink; then I went to the ladies' room. On the way back, I took a route that led me directly past Peter's booth. By now Dawn had sat down with Peter and his friend. "Why don't you join us?" Dawn said with a slight smirk. But Peter didn't say a word.

I looked straight at the nameless young woman and introduced myself, with what I hoped was icy grandeur, as Mrs. Peter Pinchbeck, as if this were a scene from *Lady Windermere's Fan*. Then I told Peter not to bother coming home.

When I got back to Greene Street, I flung all his clothes into the freight elevator and slammed down the door.

That wasn't the end, though. By September, Peter was trying to live with Daniel and me once again. I'd gone to Fire Island in August on my vacation, and Peter had come out one day to visit Daniel. I watched them walk down to the beach hand in hand, Peter with his stoop and long, lopsided lope, Daniel trotting along to keep up with his father. After we had put Daniel to bed, Peter was supposed to catch the last ferry. Instead he sat with me in the tiny backyard of the small house I'd rented and told me he'd missed us. The reason he and I had been having so much difficulty, he said, was that he found it unbearable to have no hope of showing his work. But all that was going to change, he promised me. A new gallery in SoHo had taken him on—in January he would finally have a one-man show.

Peter did seem different—some of his old boyish optimism had returned to him—and I could tell he was truly contrite, so I agreed to take him back. Despite my bitterness, I'd missed him too—missed him the way you couldn't help missing an old friend you'd fallen out with, someone who was simply part of your life. But I told myself I'd only give him one more chance.

As the New Year began in 1971, on our way back from a party, Peter and I came upon an abandoned dog, locked into a dog run on Houston Street. It was bitterly cold. The dog was whimpering as it ran in frantic circles on the icy ground. We stood outside the wire fence, calling to it. It came right over and sniffed gently at our hands. Peter and I made an instant decision to take it home.

A slender, aristocratic-looking dog with pale russet markings on its white coat and long, intelligent face, it seemed completely untroubled by memories of its previous home. When Peter took it to Fanelli's, someone told him it was an English setter; the bartender gave it a saucer of beer.

We all fell in love with that dog; Peter and I often marveled to each other that such a fantastic creature had come into our lives. Daniel insisted we call it Pongo and showered it with kisses; in the mornings he'd find it discreetly curled up at the foot of his bed. In the daytime, the dog hung out in the studio, its eyes fixed warmly on Peter as he sanded the pieces for his show and gave them their final coats of paint. When I came home from work, the dog would be awaiting me at the elevator; later it would look on as I gave Daniel his bath and flop down at my feet as I edited a manuscript, occasionally resting its speckled face against my leg. The dog seemed to have brought with it something that had been missing. It bound the three of us together with its uncomplicated affection.

Unfortunately, we only kept that dog a month. Its owner was searching for it all over the neighborhood—a friend told him he

had seen an English setter with Peter in Fanelli's. We went into mourning for a while after Peter returned it to its owner. Peter said we had to find another English setter; he started looking through the ads in the Pet section of the Sunday *Times.*

His show had opened just before we lost the dog, and Peter had seriously considered bringing it to the opening for luck. I'd seen the show before anyone else late at night right after Peter finished hanging it. I remember the feeling of walking into the brilliant whiteness of the gallery from the darkness of the streets and seeing the squares and angled shafts of wood painted in primary colors that seemed to float away from the walls, shaping the space around them with their red, yellow, and green shadows just as Peter had known they would once he'd hung his constructions in a pristine space. He opened a bottle of wine for us, and we stayed there together for a couple of hours, walking from piece to piece, unable to tear our eyes away.

That was the high point of Peter's show, which few people who could do anything for Peter came to see. The gallery owners were inexperienced, a wealthy couple trying out a new plaything. Nothing sold. Months after the work came down, an art critic wrote about Peter's "remarkable rectitude," but it was too late.

Peter seemed destroyed by disappointment. He soon lapsed into his old ways—absenting himself from the house between eleven P.M. and daybreak while I lay alternately dozing off and waking up to watch whatever was on television, suppressing a persistent fantasy of not being there when he returned.

At least I had a brand-new couch to lie upon—an elegant Scandinavian number with cocoa brown upholstery. I was thirty-five—it was time to have some upholstered furniture to sink into. There was also a new armchair in dark blue. I'd bought these things for us, as sort of an investment in the future of our marriage, with some of my first earnings from my new editorial job at McGraw-Hill, which I'd taken for the sole purpose of finally entering the middle class. But now I'd begun to equate that money with potential freedom—I could leave Peter anytime I wanted to and take care of Daniel quite well on my own.

It was no longer possible to pretend to Daniel that everything was all right. He was a very observant five-year-old. He was troubled by the fact that Peter had begun sleeping on a cot in the studio and wanted to know why his father was no longer with me in the big bed.

"Because it's too lumpy and bumpy for Daddy," I told him.

I could see Daniel didn't buy it. He climbed onto Peter's side of the mattress to test it out empirically. "It's not too lumpy and bumpy for me," he said. "I'll sleep in the big bed with you, Mom."

This offer seemed entirely too Freudian. I turned my head so Daniel wouldn't see my tears. I didn't want to deprive him of his father, but I was becoming convinced that it would hurt him even more to grow up in the cold, tense atmosphere of our household.

As a distraction for all of us that spring, especially Daniel, I found us another English setter, a half-grown puppy with a long pedigree and a high-strung disposition. It resisted all our half-hearted efforts to train it. Even taking it for a walk was difficult because it tended to lie down whenever it pleased, even in the midst of traffic as the light was changing on Houston Street. You could only get it to its feet by yanking its tail upward as truck drivers leaned out windows, venting their feelings in their colorful argot. The new dog chewed up everything in sight—shoes, books, chair legs, Daniel's favorite toys. Peter hated it, but Daniel wept whenever we talked about finding it a good home in the country. Finally, though, we put an ad in the *Times*.

We found a taker for the setter in late August, a few weeks before Daniel and I left Greene Street for an apartment on the Upper West Side, twenty-four hours after I'd found the place on my lunch hour. The Scandinavian couch went with us, but the dark blue chair was in such ruinous condition, I decided to leave it behind.

The dog had gone to work on both one night in late July when no one was in the house. Peter was away on a solo camping trip in New Mexico, trying to come to terms with the fact that I'd just told him I was having an affair with a man I'd met on Fire Island; Daniel was spending the weekend with my mother; I was out with my new boyfriend, whom I'd promised not to see in Peter's absence. When I came home the next morning, there were pieces of foam rubber all over the floor; one was still wedged between the dog's jaws. "Right," I thought with despair and with something that felt like relief. "Let it all go!"

In my bare new living room on West Seventy-ninth Street, which had dirty beige walls because I'd moved in so precipitously after a big fight with Peter that there hadn't been time to paint, I threw an Indian bedspread over the couch. Then I decided it had better lines in its authentic partly demolished state, which I disguised with a few stragetically placed kilim cushions. I kept meaning to get rid of that couch, but I had it until Daniel and I moved on.

Peter and I remained furious with each other for about six months. Once, though, when we were both feeling lonely, we went to bed for the final time, which did nothing to abate his anger or mine. He'd gotten sick of the Remington's crowd, he told me, and was now spending his nights at Max's Kansas City, a far more glamorous hangout, according to the gossip columns, where art and rock and the fashion world all converged and where, I suspected, Peter often felt like a fish out of water, though I gathered there was no shortage of extremely attractive women.

My own nights, once I'd turned out the lights in Daniel's room, were mostly spent alone on the Scandinavian couch. I was teaching myself to crochet—handicrafts were as much the rage in the 1970s as wild sexual escapades—and was making an afghan, square upon square. In the small hours of the morning, I'd often pass out, my lap filled with yellow and orange wool. When I gave up on the afghan, I briefly tried macramé. My boyfriend was a labor organizer, which seemed to necessitate spending a great deal of time in transit; a little farther uptown he had another woman he never quite managed to break up with. Still, I had no regrets about leaving Greene Street, about being out again in the world.

All over America women were walking out on their marriages, hoping to come up with some better arrangement—something more equitable, something that might bring them more ecstasy on a daily basis than life in the traditional nuclear family. It was really a national phenomenon, though not quite as widespread as the emergence of the hippies. As long as you were free, there was possibility, or at least hope.

I gave up macramé and started reading—Betty Friedan, Simone de Beauvoir, the entire works of Colette—and found reflections of myself in those books. I discovered that in the new apartment it was possible to write, if I did it very early in the morning before Daniel woke up—just for an hour, just one page or even one paragraph; one sentence that pleased me could light up the the day. I felt like a convalescent learning to walk all over again.

The first time Peter came uptown to see Daniel, he arrived clutching a small paper bag—in it was a red ball attached to a wooden paddle by a rubber band. He stood in his coat glancing around the living room as if he were afraid of being ambushed, looking extremely ill at ease when Daniel ran to him and insisted upon dragging him into his new room. Peter asked me if it was a good idea to take Daniel to Riverside Drive. Two hours later he returned him with a curt ring of the doorbell and was already escaping into the elevator by the time I opened the door. There was the sense that he had just performed some grim obligation.

I wanted something much better than that. I'd seen too much fatherlessness. Our son needed a father, a real one. And when you came down it, I thought, Daniel was all Peter really had.

A few months later, I had a lawyer draw up a separation agreement—the only thing I asked of Peter was that he spend every other weekend with Daniel. It's strange to think of that now as a demand, a condition I felt I had to insist upon, afraid that without it Peter might simply melt away. I kept hoping he'd want to fight for more time with his son.

At first those weekends must have been hard for both of them. Peter had reverted to the way he'd lived when we first met, to his spartan diet of fish cakes, hamburgers, and canned beans. Daniel's old room had disappeared when the Sheetrock walls came down. He slept in a corner of the studio on a cot—the same one Peter had attempted to stretch his long limbs out upon after abandoning the big bed. At a loss as to how to amuse a child, Peter treated Daniel like a buddy, a potential disciple—someone to play chess with, someone he could teach to look at paintings the way he did, who would sit quietly at his side at Fanelli's during intense discussions about the future of abstraction, someone who would always worry about him a little.

Daniel was the kind of a child who worried about other people. I remember him telling me when he was six that a playmate of his hated his life; "It isn't right for someone to hate his life," he said solemnly. Even before he was in his teens, he became mindful of the penalties his father paid for the stubbornness with which he went his own way.

Peter had gone back to painting on canvas a few months before we left Greene Street. Except for a piece he gave Daniel and me to hang in our new living room, the constructions from the show that had disappointed him had gone the way of the red piece he'd made for the Jewish Museum. The spatial relationships, the unseen tensions, that could be created through combinations of flat color excited him now—the endless possibilities in a repeated motif of three painted squares. Nothing in life meant more, Peter taught Daniel, than being seized by an idea that could only be

communicated through one's unceasing work. It was an unusual
education for a kid. At times Daniel wondered if his father would
ever get tired of painting his triad of squares; at times he longed
for a father who would take him fishing or play ball with him, who
wouldn't always be talking about Mondrian or Cézanne or the
Russian Constructivists. Still I can't remember one weekend when
he was reluctant to visit Peter.

During the first half dozen years of our separation, I saw little of
Peter myself. He would pick Daniel up, or I would drop him off,
and we'd talk on the phone to make arrangements. Gradually our
conversations grew longer, more cordial, though both of us remained guarded about the relationships we were having with others. Though he showed no inclination to ever marry again or even
attempt to live with anyone, Peter proved to be luckier in love
than I was.

When Daniel was around nine or ten, I began hearing the name
Maggie when he came back from his weekends. Maggie Poor, I
eventually learned, was in her early twenties, tall and beautiful, just
out of Brown University and new to New York. I heard that Maggie was an artist herself, but neither she nor Peter ever said anything about her work to me. All I knew for some time was that
Maggie was lovely to Daniel, friendly to me on the phone, convinced that Peter was a remarkable painter, and apparently innocently unaware that he was twenty years older. Whatever her own
longings were, Maggie knew better than to move in with Peter. For
over ten years she remained devoted to him. She seemed able to
laugh at Peter's idiosyncrasies, accepting them with a certain generous ruefulness until their relationship ended abruptly in the late
1980s, several years before she died of cancer at forty-three. She
told me she simply needed to be alone to find out who she was, but

she was ill by then, and I suspect she had learned there were ways in which Peter would be unable to come through for her. Although she and Peter broke up, they remained close as friends.

Peter's real forte had always been friendship—something held him back from fully entering into deep attachments, though maybe with Maggie he nearly went as far as he could. He seemed to ascribe his limitations to the requirements of his art, but perhaps he knew himself better than anyone imagined. His attachment to his son was the most enduring one he ever had. In his own way, within the boundaries that encircled his feelings, he grew into a father—not a conventional father perhaps, but a father who loved his son.

The year Daniel turned eleven, Peter and I ended up seeing a great deal of each other. Two nights a week, during that winter and spring, we would borrow a car from a friend and drive north of Manhattan to a town in Westchester called Valhalla, where there was a small hospital for children who needed long-term medical care. The hospital had been given the name Blithedale. Blithe it was not, despite lawns and trees and a lot of blond wood and glass, though it was a better place for a child than the grim ward in Mt. Sinai Hospital where Daniel had just spent three months. The day Peter and I first brought Daniel up there, I came back to the empty apartment at night and picked up the ringing phone. "Mom," Daniel said, "I can't stay here. Everyone's crazy."

But Daniel had to stay at Blithedale for the next six months if he was ever to get well. He had just been put into a body cast and was hooked up to an IV twenty-four hours a day. On one of his lower vertebrae was an excruciating swelling from a source of infection no one could identify definitively, though they called his condition osteomyelitis.

* * *

During the months that Daniel was in Mt. Sinai, there were times when I'd found myself prepared to make unimaginable bargains: "Even if he's crippled, just let him live." And I'd seen the same terror in Peter's eyes, though we'd never dared to say those exact words to each other. I wonder if Peter was even able to say them to Maggie. As for me, I was alone—thrown back to all the feelings surrounding Jim's death, which I'd thought I'd begun to let go of. I'd wake up each morning to the wild fear that I was fated to lose everyone I loved.

I'd visit Daniel by breakfast time on my way to work; when I came back in the evening, I'd usually find Peter there. His presence seemed to steady Daniel in ways that mine couldn't. My anguish must have shown, despite my attempts to hide it. Perhaps Daniel was reassured to find his father seemingly unchanged. I remember how he'd laugh at Peter's predictably scathing comments about the deplorable art on the walls of the children's ward, especially the Disney decals that they both detested. Deep in conversation, they'd walk slowly up and down the corridors together, the IV trailing behind them on its leash. I remember Peter doggedly trying to play a board game with Daniel the night a little boy with a brain tumor was in the agonized process of dying just across the hall. We could still hear him even after I got up and closed the door.

I wonder now what memories Peter had to struggle against during his visits to Mt. Sinai, then to Blithedale—things he'd seen in the Blitz that he never talked about, things that later on may have made him unable to deal with Maggie's illness. He had an eye for physical perfection, averting his gaze from what was injured or blemished. He was a deeply squeamish man.

We would never say much to each other on the drive up to Valhalla. Peter would play the radio, restlessly switching from music to the news then back to music again; I would stare out at the trees, breathing in and out, preparing myself for the shock of walking into what always seemed a netherworld, where none of the children, even Daniel in his carapace of white plaster, looked like the ones you'd normally see in the street or the park, or the shiny exuberant youngsters Daniel went to school with. Many of the children at Blithedale got around on ingenious wheeled devices, maneuvering themselves along the carefully engineered ramps. One little girl who'd had encephalitis always stood on the balcony overlooking the reception area, droning the same sentence over and over. There were babies there and teenagers, kids with cerebral palsy, kids who would die of hemophilia, a boy who'd tried to leap from one rooftop to another in Harlem and broken every bone in his body. Only a few, like Daniel, would eventually make it back into the heedless world of the healthy with the odd outsider's knowledge they'd acquired. "This isn't the real world, you know," Daniel would observe to Peter and me months later during parents' day at a summer camp in Connecticut. "Yes, it is. It's just as real," we insisted, but he gave us a look of sad skepticism.

There was one boy at Blithedale, a little older than Daniel, who never had any visitors. He was a tall blond good-looking kid, who whizzed around on a skateboard with his bad foot in a cast. He told us his bones were being eaten away by something no one had been able to diagnose and that if he ever got well, he was going to be a doctor. He'd skate right up to the little girl who stood frozen on the balcony and say, "How about a smile?" Before Blithedale, he'd been living in a group home. His own parents couldn't come to see him, he once explained to us matter-of-factly, because they were in a witness protection program.

Before he was transferred to another hospital for a series of further tests, this boy would always turn up when Peter and I visited Daniel. He'd hang out with the three of us for a while, as if to absorb a little reflected warmth for himself. Then discreetly, with a perfect sense of timing, he'd glide off on his skateboard before he outwore his welcome. I believe that when he looked at us, what he saw was a family.

It was several years before I would occasionally visit Peter at the studio. It felt off-limits, that home I'd left behind; as if in order to reenter, I'd have to force my way through an invisible membrane. I was reluctant to be confronted with my own absence, afraid of whatever residue of the marriage I'd find despite all the changes. I remember being invited by Maggie to a birthday gathering for Peter. Maybe that was what first broke the ice—drinking wine out of a cracked white coffee mug I recognized, seeing a blue pitcher I'd once used for daffodils filled with brushes soaking in turpentine, the familiar density of twilight in the thick-paned factory windows.

I felt the same strangeness whenever I went to one of the openings Peter began inviting me to in the late 1970s, because I had disappeared from the art world, which had once been so important to me, as thoroughly as I had vanished from Greene Street. By 1980, whole movements I'd paid little attention to had come and gone, each newness replacing the previous one as the important art of the moment until there seemed to be a general, self-congratulatory agreement that painting was finished. But for Peter abstract painting remained inexhaustible. He moved on from his flatly painted surfaces, his triads of soft-edged squares, from a min-imalist vocabulary he ultimately found too "subtractive." By the mid-1980s, Peter's new biomorphic images often reminded me of body parts, the spaces between them alive with a texture of brush strokes that suggested the play of light. At first I didn't quite know what to make of this work, but I could feel its power. "Mind-scapes," Peter would start calling his paintings by 1993. By then his ambition had become metaphysical—to reveal with form and color "that there is an underlying structure which unifies the exter-nal world with another world or dimension beyond perception."

Many of these new canvases were huge—too monumental in their proportions to be hung in the crowded downtown group shows where Peter displayed his work whenever he could. To me, they seemed poignant in their grandeur—the embodiments of Peter's lonely defiance of the art world. They had been executed for vast public spaces where it was unlikely Peter would ever see them hung.

Some of the openings I went to were in lofts the out-of-fashion abstract painters had rented themselves for the few weeks of their show. Friendly well-wishers trudged up the stairs; there would be a lot of inexpensive wine, and enough optimism in the air to last through dinner, generated by the sheer energy of having put up all that work so that it could be seen. Faces framed by graying hair would bob up in the crowd, attached to names that had almost slipped my mind. "What are you up to these days?" people would ask the woman they probably remembered only as Peter's ex. "Writing," I'd answer as briefly as I could. "No kidding? Publish anything?"

"This is Joyce Johnson," Peter would say, without a trace of awkwardness, introducing me to some new acquaintance of his as if he and I had never shared a name. Yet it seemed necessary to him to have me there, just as it had become necessary to me not to lose track of Peter, to touch base with him every now and then. However we had once disappointed each other, we went way back, we shared a son. We were both old enough and had lost enough to value continuity.

Maybe there were women in Peter's life after Maggie, but I was never aware of a particular woman, no significant name kept coming up in conversation. By the late 1980s, he had a steady part-time teaching job in a community college that paid him just barely enough to get along. Occasionally he'd get a grant or someone would buy a painting. In the summers he found ways to go abroad, staying with painters he knew in France, visiting cousins in England on his mother's side of the family whom he hadn't seen for more than twenty years. To my surprise, he developed an affection for England; sometimes he talked about retiring there, going on the dole, getting a place in Brighton near his cousins. By then we were both in our fifties—on the verge of becoming old. Whenever I thought about Peter's old age, I felt scared for him.

I began making sure he came to dinner on Thanksgiving and Christmas. He'd arrive with small gifts, clumsily wrapped—a Beethoven quartet, a jar of lime marmalade, bars of French soap—favoring things that would be used up. I still have the last bar of soap he gave me. Sometimes I'd suggest he spend a week or two with Daniel in my new house in Vermont when I had to be away to teach at a summer writing program.

He always marked his birthdays, organizing dinners for himself with Daniel and me and painter friends he felt close to in cheap Indian restaurants in the East Village, spaghetti joints on the edge of SoHo, the Cornelia Street Café. His birthday, eerily enough, was December 9—the same day Jim had died. I'd usually present Peter with a new shirt—I still knew the length of his sleeves. He began to put on weight, and his stoop became more pronounced. But he still looked handsome in his baggy paint-stained khaki pants and secondhand tweed jackets. After his hair went white, his eyebrows seemed startlingly dark and fierce. Older women tended to stare at him, but he didn't stare back.

Though much of her work exists only on paper in drawings of delicate, fractured, vessel-like shapes, Maggie Poor was a sculptor. I saw her eloquent white organlike pieces for the first time in 1996 in her memorial show. "Being-as-vessel," she had described them, "the frail house of consciousness linked to the vessels of the dissection room." In an essay written in 1992, included in the catalog, Maggie spoke of wanting "to move deeper and deeper" into the opposite of emotional armoring: "to express intimacy, vulnerability, tenderness. Increasingly, my work addresses exposure and fragility, the passion and tenacity of survival . . . the paradox of

shedding armor to find a truer, pliant strength within." Was there
a message for Peter hidden in the text?

In 1993 he, too, was thinking a great deal about the nature of
being as he put together a small group show to be called *Presence
and Absence.* "Abstract painting," he declared confidently in the
catalog, "is a window into being because its freedom from associa-
tive subject matter permits it to evoke the unseen, the otherness of
being."

Just before ending the essay, Peter wrote: "What is ultimately
sought—a meaning beyond appearances, a glimpse of the eternal
present behind the continuous passing and the ongoing absence of
the daily flow."

The daily flow was Peter's enemy. More and more he turned his
back to it, found ways of shutting it out. He stopped trying to interest dealers and constructed his own art world of four or five
like-minded artists. They'd gather on Friday afternoons at Caffe
Dante on MacDougal Street for intense philosophical discussions
about the reinvention of abstract painting Peter was convinced
they were setting in motion. I imagine him rising reluctantly from
the table, putting on his coat, stepping outside into reality, crossing
Houston Street into the neighborhood artists like him had created,
which money was making unrecognizable. I imagine Peter walking, sometimes in a rage, past the galleries that had never shown
him and were now about to disappear from SoHo altogether, past
women with Prada shopping bags, groups of European tourists,
windows displaying the superfluous goods of conspicuous con-
sumption. Or maybe managing to see none of these things—only
the eternal present of the painting he is hurrying back to, purple
looming up in a cloud of yellow, a sudden incursion of red . . .

When he gets home, he makes himself a hamburger, then goes back to his work.

Sometimes after leaving a party, Daniel would find himself in SoHo late at night. "I would detour by his block," he wrote in an essay about his father published in *Art Forum* in 2002, "to see the light shining in his window. I would feel oddly secure in the thought that he was up in his loft working, revolving like a planet through his self-created cosmology."

Time overtook Peter sooner than anyone expected—as if it had been quietly stalking him, not close at his heels but back several paces, until entropy suddenly made it accelerate.

He came up to Vermont to visit me in the summer of '96, very relieved to be escaping the August heat of New York. I had last seen him in May, but somehow he seemed different, agitated yet slower moving. In fact, he preferred to move as little as possible, unless we were going somewhere in the car. He occupied the settee on the porch, smoked cigar after cigar, asked for innumerable cups of coffee and glasses of iced tea, and complained as usual about the absence of the *New York Times*. Carpentry didn't interest him this year, though he bought me a hook in a hardware store from which to hang a bird feeder. Nor did he feel like working in the garden, which he'd always particularly enjoyed, especially big, vigorous operations like planting bushes; one summer he'd said that pruning the branches of an apple tree felt almost like doing sculpture. At all times he kept a pencil and pad of paper near him, but he hardly made a mark on it.

Instead he talked and wanted me to stop everything and listen to him, though what he was mostly bent on communicating was maddeningly detailed accounts of each movie he'd seen lately, each novel he'd read. I'd always found enduring the retelling of plots a kind of mental torture, so after a while I'd only pretend to listen, emitting the occasional obligatory "uh-huh," excusing myself at times to do something in the kitchen, where Peter would relentlessly follow me. He was in the middle of a book about John Ruskin and was currently fascinated by the strange forms repressed sexuality had taken during the late Victorian period; he could talk about Ruskin all day long. What was wrong? I wondered. Had he become so unused to having someone to talk to that now he had to drown me in the sound of his voice?

What I had come to love most about being in the country was its silence. You could sink into that silence, let it enfold you like velvet, once you stopped resisting it. There were mornings when I was alone on the porch and the light had achieved a perfect balance, when I would look up from my writing to watch birds flying back and forth to the feeder and feel that I wanted nothing more. I was sixty-one, finally growing into my solitude. It had been many years since Daniel had left home, since my last love affair—a long passionate one corroded by secrecy—had sputtered out. I still sometimes succumbed to the panic of nonbeing. Did you exist if there was no witness? I'd stare at the woods surrounding my house and know that if I walked into them and fell or lost my way, it might be weeks before anyone realized I was missing. But then I'd right myself. There was something about nature as well as work that kept me company.

I'd make another pitcher of iced tea for Peter and carry it out to the porch, and think, "No, I could certainly never live with anyone again." His demanding, needy presence seemed to fill the small house, leaving little room for me. I wanted him to make his own damn bed, pulling the covers smooth for once; I was becoming

intensely irritated by the way anything he did in the kitchen—
even boiling water—involved a trail of crumpled paper towels.
"Why is it necessary to kill so many trees?" I found myself saying.

One night when I wanted to listen to a program on NPR, Peter
again started going on about Ruskin. Intending to sound tactful, I
couldn't help interrupting—"Look, would you mind telling me
the rest of that after the news?"—and immediately realized I'd
blindsided him without meaning to.

He knew me well enough to hear what I wasn't saying. "You
should pay attention to me even when you're bored," he yelled. I'd
forgotten his black temper, his capacity for rage.

"I don't think so," I said acidly, though I was still angry with
myself for hurting him. But then he did the wounding. "You're
hard," he said, "and cold. No wonder no one likes you." I remember feeling dumbfounded, wondering whether there were any
grains of truth in the way Peter saw me. Had I lost something essential, closed myself off?

Our whole argument was unfortunate, erupting for ancient reasons after so many years of peace. But whatever we'd broken
couldn't be fixed that night. The following morning Peter packed
his bag and asked me to drive him to the train.

I felt raw and bewildered after he was gone. For weeks the porch
smelled of his cigars.

By the time I saw him next, waiting in the hallway outside my
apartment, handing me his two customary bottles of Beaujolais
Nouveau as he caught his breath, he looked years older. Was it the
dark blue of the overcoat—the handsome secondhand overcoat,
bought in Vermont, in which he could pass for a banker, I'd told
him the day we found it—that made his face seem whiter than his
hair?

It was Thanksgiving again. All fall we'd avoided each other, only talking briefly the day I finally called to invite him to the dinner. "Daniel will be there, of course," I'd said nervously, "and the usual suspects."

There had been a pause in which our quarrel stirred in the background, still unresolved. But he and I had never been in the business of talking things out—it was too late for that to change.

He'd cleared his throat, then said, "Sure, I'll come. I'll bring the wine."

Up to that moment, I'd been thinking of calling Thanksgiving off, not bothering with it that year—the shopping, the hours of cooking. Why was it that the whole effort would have seemed pointless if Peter had told me he couldn't make it?

He was breathing hard as he hung up his coat, like someone who had been climbing stairs, yet he'd taken the elevator. At dinner he mentioned that he'd had the flu for weeks; it had started in September, and he was surprised how long it was taking him to get over it. "Next year get a shot early," people at the table advised him. He carved the turkey, as he always did, though he offered to let Daniel do the honors. "I'm making a mess of this," he said cheerfully, hacking the meat into thick slices. When the platter was passed around, he took very little for himself. I looked across the table as Peter bent over his plate and saw how the flesh of his face sagged off the bones.

He had always been so strong, hauling loads of two-by-fours in and out of the elevator, moving enormous canvases around with one gloved hand on the crossbars of the stretchers. Whenever I worried about Peter, whenever I tried to prepare myself for some crisis that might confront him in his old age, the disaster I imagined was that he'd run out of money, lose his teaching job—or worse, lose the loft due to some change in rent regulations or the landlord's growing desire to profit more from his building. Where would Peter go with any other loft so impossibly beyond his reach? What would become of the paintings? How would he survive being crammed into a tiny apartment in the outer reaches of the boroughs, where he could no longer do his work?

I never said so to Peter, but I knew I would help him as much as I could. Still, how far was I prepared to go? Each time he came to Vermont, I'd ask myself that troubling question. But I'd never imagined that all of a sudden, when he was only sixty-five, Peter would simply run out of health.

Only a few weeks after Thanksgiving, Daniel called me. "Dad's in the hospital," he said. The "flu" Peter had been unable to recover from was an infection that had damaged his heart valve. It was possible to have an operation, but it was risky, and he had decided against it.

I went down to Greene Street after the hospital let Peter go. Daniel was there running errands, trying to take care of him, looking stricken—I could tell he was feeling out of his depth. I'd been to the studio last the year before for one of Peter's birthday celebrations—I remembered him pouring out tumblers of wine for everyone, tearing the wrappings off his presents, before we all trooped out to a restaurant. The loft hadn't seemed bleak to me then as we stood with our glasses in a small bright clearing Peter had made in the midst of the shifting landscape of painted shapes and colors that made the dingy walls dissolve. This time different canvases were up, large ones Peter's illness had interrupted, but I could barely look at them. I saw the tattered army blankets on the thin mattress, the unmopped bathroom floor, the empty refrigerator, the desk piled with notes, sketches, unpaid bills. The living space had never seemed so small, a shrinking island surrounded by decades of unsold works. And Peter was shrinking, his strength gone, struggling to breathe as he lay on the bed, but I knew he was already calculating how soon he could get on his feet to paint.

He lay propped up on the bed because there was really no comfortable place for him to sit and listened patiently as I told him he'd have to learn to eat differently—no hamburgers, no salt. He could learn to cook vegetables for himself, I said, make salads. I tried to convince him it was very easy to make a salad, but he had a baffled, bad-boyish look on his face that I recognized—if a woman made him a salad, then he would eat it.

I washed all the dishes that had been left in the sink, then went out to the health food store on Spring Street and returned with several prepared dinners. Later that week I sent down an armchair I'd bought for Peter in a thrift shop, so that he could stay out of bed several hours a day. The armchair had off-white textured upholstery, almost pristine, and a matching ottoman. In the studio they gleamed like invading aliens.

He declared himself better, though walking a few too many blocks still took his breath away. I don't remember him complaining or talking about feeling scared. If you spoke to him on the phone, he'd sound cheerful, even excited—the work was going well, which seemed to be all that really mattered. He positioned the chair and the ottoman so that they faced the painting wall.

The obliviousness in which Peter cocooned himself had become very troubling to Daniel. How could his father go on producing painting after painting at this time in his life without the slightest hope of success? I understood why Peter kept on—the pure joy he found in the act—yet I too found it painful to look at the new canvases. The knowledge of how much Peter had given up for them got in the way. I dreaded the group shows that seemed so pathetic now, so futile.

I couldn't bring myself to go to the latest one, on view in an office building all the way downtown on Broad Street. When the drab, cheaply printed catalog arrived in the mail, I put it away, scarcely glancing at it, without reading the short introductory essay by Peter that revealed an important further development in his thinking:

"The 'abstract' is perhaps a misnomer for these constructions, because to abstract in painting is to dematerialize the world, to reduce it to decorative elements, whereas these images are concretions, means of making feeling and form tangible."

I also missed the remarkably serene statement that appeared opposite a blurry black-and-white photo of the painting entitled *Locus* that Peter had contributed to the show:

"Ultimately it does not matter when the painting was made, what style it represents, or what the medium is, although these are obviously concerns of the painter. All that matters is that the viewer is visually transported."

The Number 5 bus begins its long drowsy journey from SoHo to the Upper West Side at the corner of West Broadway and Houston Street, a stop that has become as significant to me as the one on Grand Street and the Bowery. I can never wait there for the Number 5 without reminding myself, all over again, of Peter's absence—a fact I should have absorbed by now, yet still haven't quite committed to memory. This was where Peter would usually say good-bye to me whenever I came downtown to see him.

Over the years Houston Street had become the northern boundary of Peter's world—Daniel and I often used to tease him about his maddening reluctance to go beyond it. But after Peter got sick, we didn't joke about it anymore and no longer attempted to coax him a little farther uptown to have Sunday brunch with us in the Village. Instead we'd arrange to meet him only a couple of blocks from the studio. We referred to these brunches with ironic pride as our "family ritual." When Daniel arrived one Sunday with Laura Hoffmann, a beautiful young woman who had become very important to him, Peter and I had the feeling our family was about to increase.

Now and then, during those last three years, Peter and I would have what I can only call "dates"—because there was something circumspect and shy, oddly old-fashioned, about them, as if we were turning back the clock and starting all over again as the chaste, conservative couple we'd never been when we were young. Usually we'd dine in the same restaurant, Kelley and Ping, an Asian noodle place right on Greene Street—a few times we even went to the movies—then Peter would see me to that bus stop, where we'd awkwardly kiss each other, and I'd watch him slowly cross Houston Street alone.

One night in 1999, in a great departure from our usual routine, I arrived at Peter's studio without much warning with a delegation of eight writers from Vietnam, who were visiting New York as guests of PEN. Earlier that evening I'd been helping my friend Susan Brownmiller, who had recently published a book on Vietnam, entertain them at her apartment in the West Village. They were middle-aged men, heavy smokers in baggy suits; a very long time ago they had all fought against us in the war. After a few days of being shepherded to tourist sites and listening to translated speeches about democracy, they seemed weary and politely glum, as if they were beginning to realize they might go back to their country without ever seeing the real thing, however they defined it, or at least some very small piece of the real New York. I asked their translator whether the writers would be interested in visiting the studio of an American painter I happened to know personally. They all brightened up when she put it to them, and I made the call.

Within an hour and half, we were all standing in front of 69 Greene Street as a cold December rain drizzled down on us. The Vietnamese looked doubtfully at the old industrial building—had they been brought to a factory? Obviously they had no idea of what to expect. Then the door that led out onto the loading platform opened and Peter appeared, warmly smiling and shaking hands as his guests passed through the entranceway as if he had been welcoming delegations all his life.

The big antiquated elevator was a wonder to the Vietnamese; when the heavy door crashed down, there was nervous laughter. Stepping cautiously out into the loft, they seemed gratified to be having an adventure very much off the beaten path. I'm trying to imagine Peter's studio through their eyes—the sheer size of it, the hundreds of paintings stored there in racks or propped against walls, the scale of some of the canvases, the extraordinary combinations of color. Perhaps they were also struck by the puzzling austerity of the surroundings; the artist who had spent his lifetime working in this huge space was surely far from rich. One of the Vietnamese tapped me on the shoulder; he wanted me to convey to the host that in his youth he too had been a painter.

I was a little astonished when Peter produced a bottle of pear brandy, which he measured out into small paper cups for each of his guests. It was an unknown drink for me, though I had once seen an orchard in France where pears were ripening inside bottles. I wasn't the only one surprised by the power of the first sip—it tasted not only of pear, I thought, but of captured sunlight.

By now the atmosphere was becoming festive. The Vietnamese writers were smiling and making toasts, eagerly giving the translator questions for Peter. They had forgotten the rain and darkness, the strangeness of waiting outside on an unknown street in America. As they savored the last of their brandy, Peter began pulling canvases out of the racks, moving them into the light one after the other. That night he seemed strong and tireless. Remembering to

pause intermittently to let the translator catch up, he explained
how he did his work, told the story of how he had come to America from England forty years ago to become an abstract painter, as
his visitors listened, mesmerized. I was captivated myself, as if I
were hearing all this for the first time. I had never known Peter to
be more eloquent, never seen him more entirely in his element.
Whatever language may have eluded translation, I knew he was
communicating his passionate longing to open eyes, to share his
visions with anyone who cared to look, which was, I realized, the
kind of love stored up inside him that he'd always had to give.

Peter never visited me again in Vermont. The subtle boundary line
of our relationship had become as clear to us as Houston Street.
For a couple of summers I received postcards from small art
colonies where Peter was able to paint but felt cooped up without a
car and was lonely, I suspected, surrounded by younger people. As
the summer of 2000 approached, he seemed to have nothing lined
up. "Dad really needs to get out of the city this year," said Daniel,
who was living in SoHo now with Laura and seeing more of his
father.

I felt a twinge of guilt. Perhaps I would let Peter have my house
for a couple of weeks and just arrange to be elsewhere, but I knew
him well enough to think he might turn the offer down.

He called me one morning late in May—"Joyce, I need your
advice." He sounded breathless, but it seemed to be from excitement. I was astonished when he told me he was considering buying a place in the Catskills. The house was tiny, Peter said, and had
been painted pink, which was unfortunate, but it had a woodstove
and could be lived in into October. He could do some useful
thinking there and manage to paint some small works, and he'd
even be among friends, because the house was in a co-op, an old

bungalow colony some artists he knew had bought into. The artists were part of Peter's small group of die-hard abstract painters. "There's a pine tree in the yard," he added, "of considerable size."

The situation sounded right for him in every way, and the house cost very little, only fifteen thousand dollars. Peter asked me anxiously, did I think it would be a good investment? and I thought of how little money he'd managed to put aside toward his old age. *Investment* was a word seldom heard in his vocabulary.

"I'd like to leave something for Daniel," he said with a strange urgency.

I took that in for a moment, then my thoughts rebounded from what it implied as I tried to imagine Daniel and Laura spending weekends in a bungalow colony of middle-aged artists. "Are you really sure," I asked Peter, "that Daniel would want to go there?"

He agreed that he wasn't, but as he'd found out over the years, there was nothing like having a small place of your own, something no landlord could take from you. He said he worried about Daniel, the precariousness of Daniel's life as a writer.

"The point is, Peter," I said slowly, "is this something *you* want?"

He caught his breath, then admitted almost with shame, "Yes. Yes, *I* want it."

I found myself unable to advise him to proceed cautiously.

"Peter," I said to him, "I want you to have that place."

I told him I'd lend him the money for the down payment and not to worry at all about rushing to pay me back.

I was leaving town soon for the summer, and I'd just published a new book, so I didn't get down to Greene Street. As the purchase of the house went forward, I talked to Peter almost daily on the phone. When I mentioned I'd be giving a reading in a bookstore on Astor Place, to my surprise Peter said he'd definitely make it—he'd never gone to any of my readings—and that night was the last time I saw him. There was a dinner afterward. He sat at the other end of the long table, but he walked out of the restaurant with me when it was over, and we said good night hurriedly on the sidewalk as I climbed into a cab.

I seem to be haunted by casual good-byes. I even said good-bye to my mother on the street. We were standing outside her doctor's office as she leaned on the arm of the woman who took care of her. "I'm a little tired," she murmured. "I'll come by tomorrow," I promised.

It was a summer of too many scorching days and not nearly enough rain, but all summers seemed to be like that now, though everyone still commented upon "the unusual weather." I was glad Peter was up in the Catskills. He'd been able to move right into his house, even though the technicalities of owning it had not been completed. Two old friends, artists who were steadfast admirers of his work, had also lent him money.

He called me a couple of times from a neighbor's phone to tell me about his progress. He had thrown out much of the furniture that had been left there, he was about to paint one room white, he had bought himself an old Dodge van that ran pretty well. There was a porch big enough for a chair, or maybe even a hammock like the one I had on mine.

An envelope filled with snapshots arrived in the mail. The bungalow was so small that Peter looked entirely out of scale standing on the lower of its two front steps. The pink paint was the color of cotton candy, and the Dodge appeared to be a weird, only somewhat darker shade. It was the last kind of place you could have imagined as the object of Peter's yearning, yet he was beaming.

He called me on a Saturday afternoon to announce that he'd finally gotten his own phone. It was the very end of August. In Vermont the fields were full of goldenrod and asters, I told him. He was returning to the city by bus the following day because his classes were about to start, but he intended to spend weekends at his house as long as the weather held out. I asked him how things were going. He said he was fine, he had everything he needed. He'd picked up an old wooden kitchen table at a yard sale, the perfect fit for a space he'd cleared by a window, and that was where he'd been working on a series of small paintings on paper. It had been quiet all week because his friends had gone back to New York, but the quiet had been good for him. "I think I'm on the verge of something," he said.

Daniel was in the Nevada desert, covering the Burning Man Festival for *Rolling Stone*. Peter asked if I'd heard from him, but I reminded him there were no phones.

We talked for a long while. He was full of ideas about enlarging the house, first making the porch big enough so that he could work out there too, then maybe the rest of the place, slowly building outward.

"As long as you have the infrastructure," I remember saying.

"Yes," Peter said, "that's right. I'll get started next summer. Maybe I'll sell a painting or two in the meantime."

There was a lightness, a warmth in his voice as he spoke to me that I hadn't heard for years. In fact, there was something different about the way I was talking to him, too—a sudden airiness, as if the constraints that had always been there had blown away.

Finally, although I hated to get off the phone, I reminded Peter that we were running up his bill. But there was more he wanted to say.

"You have to see this place. I really want you to come up here."

"I'll come," I said. "I'll be back before October."

* * *

I saw Peter's house only a couple of weeks later, drove up there in the middle of September with Daniel and Laura and Peter's friend Tom Evans. As Peter had said, it was an easy two-hour ride—we crossed the George Washington Bridge; then a series of broad

highways with shoulders as well manicured as suburban lawns propelled us onward to an exit not far over the state line. There the road shrank to two lanes. Rounded mountains rose across vistas of yellow stubble fields that had yielded their corn. We drove through Monticello, New York, a dejected-looking town of used-tire and check-cashing places and discount food markets. Tom, who had been doing most of the talking during the ride, pointed out a diner where Peter had been fond of going for pancakes.

When we drove into "Bungalow City," I recognized the old pinkish Dodge van parked in the grass near the gate. All the bungalows except Peter's were painted sensible dark greens and browns. The one he had bought was the smallest—it looked even tinier than it had in the snapshots. Tom went to find a key, then let us inside.

When the door opened, we stepped into a greenish old-fashioned kitchen that looked as if it dated from the early 1950s; adjoining it was the other room—the one Peter had painted white. The fresh paint still had its gleam and a faint dry odor. There was a single wooden chair—this too had been made white, as had the table under the window. The dark cover on the narrow bed had been pulled taut. It was as still in there as a chapel—nothing to draw the eye but a glory of little paintings, as luminous as a swarm of butterflies, tacked to the white walls.

After looking at each one, Daniel suddenly walked out of the house and sat down by himself on the brown grass under the pine tree. Laura waited for a moment, then went to him.

I wandered about in Peter's house as uneasily as a trespasser. Not knowing what I was searching for, I pulled open a closet. Old shirts and trousers hung there, and a sweater I'd given Peter for one of his birthdays. The kitchen cabinet was full of canned beans and Campbell's soup and a shelf of empty pill bottles.

Late in the afternoon when we took down the paintings, carefully prying out the tacks, the white room became small again, and we could no longer feel Peter there.

He had died in his loft not long after he got home. Until Daniel came looking for him, his body lay there for a week.

"I really want you to come up here."

*I've often played back the last words Peter said to me. They hang in the air like the smoke from one of his cigars that I sometimes think I smell when I walk out onto the porch in Vermont. We were never meant to be husband and wife, but despite our insoluble separateness, I know some measure of recognition and tenderness passed between us.*

*I still ask myself whether he knew he was dying that summer. At first, the thought that he must have was unbearable to me. No one was with him, I kept thinking, and in his aloneness I saw my own. But then, when Daniel and I were going through Peter's papers, we found a newspaper clipping he had obviously filed away for future reference in a folder marked "Bungalow Deal." It was an article about a house in the Arizona desert built from salvaged materials and earth and glass, with a tilted translucent roof that brought the western sky inside. The interior—25 × 100, like Peter's loft on Greene Street—was exquisitely empty, as if waiting to be filled with innumerable canvases. I think of Peter there in that space as he worked at the table in his bungalow, doors flying open in his mind to everything he was going to paint next.*

*He died before he could outlive his imagination. Any artist would wish for such an ending. I would like to be as lucky and as brave.*